MAREK KOMAR

Mind without Mind

Using Zen And The Science of Flow to Get Out of Your Own Way, And Perform at Your Best

First edition

ISBN: 978-1-7775191-0-0

Editing by Melissa Kirk
Cover art by Adam Renvoize

This book was professionally typeset on Reedsy.
Find out more at reedsy.com

To my parents. Without you, none of this would have been possible.

To my wife. My number one fan who keeps me going.

"Because the mountains we climb are not made only of rock and ice but also dreams and desire. The mountains we climb are mountains of the mind."

– Robert MacFarlane

Contents

INTRODUCTION

We all seek ways to get out of our own heads. We don't like being there most of the time. We overthink things, don't trust ourselves, and make our lives more difficult than they should be. This is not an ideal mindset to have heading into a competition or performance. Often we waste the mental capacity we need in order to perform well by worrying about the wrong things, ruminating about past mistakes, or looking ahead to the future to an outcome that has not yet happened.

Once in a while though, seemingly out of nowhere, we do manage to get out of our own way and the ceaseless inner chatter and self-analysis comes to a brief halt. We stop caring about what others might say, what we look like, what the result might be, and instead allocate our precious energy and attention to what is actually in front of us and within our control. This is the place where we feel at our best and perform at our best: no overthinking required.

In the age of big data, complicated metrics, and over-analysis, there is something missing in how we look at personal performance. Clubs put young athletes through combines and camps, reducing each performance metric to a number which we then compare to the rest, hoping to discover the next big star. We have honed the science of physical performance and believe that we can predict who will come out on top.

Yet no metric on jump height, bench press, or sprint speed will ever correlate with how a person will perform when the chips are down, when they're in the final minute of the big game, their team is behind, and they are completely exhausted. These numbers cannot predict the courage and self-awareness that it takes to bounce back from a defeat when your fans, your coach, or the entire internet are asking for your head. What really matters is learning to conquer the biggest battle we will ever face: the one against ourselves.

This book is your guide to getting you out of your own way and starting to train the most valuable tool you have in your arsenal: your mind. Too often the mind is overlooked in sports performance. We tend to think great moments boil down to luck, or just sheer physical effort. Although both have an important role, this attitude completely overlooks the key aspects of performance that occur in the three pounds of nervous issue within one's skull: the trainable variables of calmness, focus, confidence, the ability to let go of mistakes, communication skills, leadership, and other key factors. It is not only the body that pushes the limits of human performance, but also the mind. The two are not separate from one another.

This book is my attempt to shine some light on what I see as missed opportunities to become one's absolute best. This is not your typical performance psychology book, filled with inspirational quotes (well, there are a few), passages on "visualizing greatness", and a step-by-step guide to becoming mentally tough. From my perspective, there are no guaranteed recipes for success. There is only the awareness of what success means to you and your personal journey to happiness and well-being through the medium of performance. This book is intended to leave you with not only a better understanding of mental training, but also with practical tools to implement in your own life.

I've developed these tools using current research in the performance and psychological sciences as well as through my work with clients in my role as a Mental Performance Consultant with various athletes, individuals, teams, and organizations through my consulting business, Flow Performance.

FLOW AND 'NO MIND'

Our understanding of the psychology of human behaviour has grown over the years. We now know that peak experiences in competition and performance are not mystical nonsense, but rather something known as a *state of flow*. Having a mind without mind, which I will discuss in Chapter 1, is the key to achieving flow. In flow we are not in our own way, judging this or that, but rather seamlessly moving from one moment to the next effortlessly.

In Part one of this book, "The Science of Flow" I will define and explore flow through a more scientific lens, looking at the decades of research on this experience of having no mind.

Part two: "Training for Flow", I will introduce a framework for training yourself to achieve this flow state more frequently through what I call Mental Performance Training, or MPT for short. Here I blend the science of peak performance with philosophical insight I've learned both through working with individuals on the path to mastery, as well as my own personal journey navigating these states of mind.

Part three will then discuss "Recovering from Flow" where I explore the concept of recovery, specifically learning to navigate the strenuous water of high performance by stepping back onto shore every once in a while.

NOT ONLY FOR ATHLETES

Although my focus in this book is primarily on the modern-day athlete, the skills I cover are not limited to this group. After all, life is a performance, and we are all performers. Whether you are a corporate/executive athlete, musician, student, or parent, you may find something useful here. Whatever your performance goal, I hope this will be a guide for you on your personal journey of achieving peak experiences more often. By no means do I declare myself the expert. After all, you know yourself better than anyone else ever will. But since you're already here, give it a shot and see where it takes you. All that you need is already within you.

Throughout the book there are numerous worksheets and exercises which can be completed using the workbook available for download at www.flowperformancepsych.com/workbook-download.

The password to access the file is *NoMind2021*.

I

PART ONE: THE SCIENCE OF FLOW

"It's not the mountain we conquer, but ourselves."
– Sir Edmund Hilary

1

MIND AND NO MIND

What is the mind? Is it the soft tissue inside your skull? Is it the billions of neurons firing within your brain? What constitutes a thought? A feeling? These are all questions beyond the scope of this book. Sorry to disappoint. But something happened when you read those words. Within your own mind there was activity. Perhaps you were intrigued by the questions. Or maybe you questioned purchasing this book. In any case, there was something happening inside your mind.

The study of how we interpret what lies between our own two ears has intrigued me for a very long time, and I am not alone in this pursuit. The interaction between mind and body is a question that many scientists, psychologists and philosophers have pondered over the centuries. "Know thyself" was said to be inscribed on the Temple of Apollo at Delphi in Ancient Greece. But how does one really get to know oneself? Is this really something that we can achieve?

As much as we understand the science behind psychological states, there are some states of mind that are very hard to grasp, measure, and comprehend. For example, the feeling of time slowing down during a competition, or how Formula 1 drivers talk about being "one" with the car and the road. Colin O'Brady, an adventure athlete who was the first person in history to cross Antarctica solo, unsupported and unaided (A 932-mile expedition in 54 days!) has this to say about a state of mind he experienced during the expedition:

> *"I ended up being in this timeless, spaceless place in my mind of true high performance that was almost like the most deepest, peaceful meditative state that I could possibly imagine. It was very profound and beautiful to get there in my mind."* [1]

These states of mind are difficult to understand through a scientific lens, but they are still worth exploring. After all, they are meant to be experienced rather than dissected. In my view we should never confuse knowledge with experience.

If we are to perform at our best, it is essential that we get better at understanding our own mind and what makes it function at its most optimal. We all have different objectives and unique experiences that shape how we think, feel, and participate in the world. You can read all the self-help books you want, but the reality is that every book is written from someone else's perspective on mastering their own life, which may or may not apply to yours. But what we can lean on is the ancient wisdom and modern-day science to guide us with our journey of mental mastery.

THE WISDOM OF NO MIND

For a long time, I have been fascinated with studying the mind and its role in performance. What sparked this fascination is my discovery of the Japanese concept of *mushin no shin*, a Zen Buddhist expression meaning: *mind without mind*. It is also referred to as the state of "no-mindness", shortened into *mushin*, or *no-mind*. It is a mind not fixed or occupied by thought or emotion and thus open to everything. As philosopher Alan Watts once put it:

"It is a state of wholeness in which the mind functions freely and easily, without the sensation of a second mind or ego standing over it with a club."[2]

No-mind does not mean a mindless state. Nor does it mean that there is literally no mind, but rather that there is no conscious activity of the mind that is too pre-occupied with itself in ego-consciousness. In other words, a state of no-mind is a free mind that is not restricted by ideas, desires, and images that distract from the present moment experience. No-mind is a practical transcendence from the everyday mind, without departing from the everydayness of the world. [3]

Ancient samurai were said to have rigorously trained in order to reach a state of no-mind. In some ways, they were the first that we know of in modern history to have a formal mental training program. Having a state of no-mind was essential to survival. Fixating on doubt or fear in the heat of battle would mean certain death.

Mind without mind is achieved when a person's mind is free from thought: the internal chatter of the mind, whether in anger, fear, or ego. There is an absence of wandering thought and judgment, so the person is totally free to act and respond to a situation without hesitation and without disturbance. The individual reaches a point where they do not rely on what they think the next move should be, but rather trust their natural instinct to take over in an effortless effort. The legendary Zen master Takuan Sōhō describes it this way:

"The mind must always be in the state of 'flowing,' for when it stops anywhere that means the flow is interrupted and it is this interruption that is injurious to the well-being of the mind. In the case of the swordsman, it means death. When the swordsman

stands against his opponent, he is not to think of the opponent,
nor of himself, nor of his enemy's sword movements. He just
stands there with his sword which, forgetful of all technique, is
ready only to follow the dictates of the subconscious. The man has
effaced himself as the wielder of the sword. When he strikes, it is
not the man but the sword in the hand of the man's subconscious
that strikes."[4]

NO-MIND AND THE ATHLETE

Now this concept may seem like an outlandish idea for the modern athlete, but consider this: how often have you found yourself lost in thought while you were participating in a competition or even in a workout? It happens quite often that our mind drifts either to the past—such as to a previous mistake—or towards the future, worried about something that could go wrong. In fact, a study out of Harvard University found that our mind wanders around 47% of the time during waking consciousness[5]. That is almost half of your day spent ruminating about the past or caught up in thinking about the future! This kind of mental wandering and preoccupation is detrimental to peak performance. What we've found instead is that complete and utter presence are what contributes the most to proficient performance: a mind that is totally aware and in tune with its surroundings and to what needs to be done now rather than on what has happened in the past or what may happen in the future.

If you have watched the movie *The Last Samurai*, you might recall a scene where the main character Nathan Algren (Tom Cruise) was sparring with a partner and was visibly having some trouble. What followed was a quick dialogue with him and another soldier, Nobutada:

Nobutada- *"Please forgive, too many mind."*

Nathan- *"Too many mind?"*

Nobutada- *"Hai. Mind the sword, mind the people watching, mind the enemy, too many mind... No mind."*[6]

MIND   **NO MIND**   **MIND**

No mind is the space in between negative and positive mind. Essentially, both ends of the spectrum are a distraction. Negative mind could be a preoccupation with a mistake or negative comment. This pulls us away from the present. Similarly, being overly excited about a goal you just scored can take you away from the fact that there are still 10 minutes left to be played in the game. This is why many teams are most vulnerable to getting scored on when they themselves have just scored.

For the best performance, where we should be instead is that place in the middle: the place where we are not pulled in one direction or the other but rather respond to the moment-by-moment demands of competition. It is only when we are fully "here and now" that we are most receptive to moving fluidly, with the mind and body in sync. Hence, it is a mind that is without mind.

A QUICK STORY

To understand and appreciate the importance of having no mind, it helps to have experienced moments of adversity and challenge. My first real experience with having a mind without mind happened during an innocent summer camp table tennis tournament when I was thirteen years old. I was playing in the final game against none other than my best friend. The match was not going well for me to say the least, as not only was I down by one set, but I also had ten points to catch up to, leaving my friend on match point, potentially winning the tournament and all the pride that goes with it. This meant that to even have a chance at a comeback, I had to win at *least ten points in a row*, without making any mistakes. I had two options: call it a day and let my opponent win or try my best to go out with some pride. With my opponent being my best friend with whom I have had a competitive history, failure was not really an option.

I chose to stick it out and hope for the best. With nothing to lose, I decided to just play it point by point. I told myself: *let's just try and win the next point, nothing else.* He was the one with something to lose here, and knowing him from childhood I knew he was already focused on the celebration. I'll spare you the exciting play-by-play of these two 13-year-old ping pong prodigies but, point by point I found myself getting closer to even. 8 points to go, 6 points to go... My opponent was starting to get visibly nervous and made more and more mistakes. As for me, I just stuck to the game plan: focus on the point in front of you. My mouth was shut the entire set. I was in what athletes call "the zone."

20-19. I was one point away from doing the impossible. My opponent was distraught at allowing my comeback. *Can I actually do this?* I thought, but quickly reminded myself to get back to the present. My opponent made another unforced error, and the comeback was complete. 20-20... The crowd goes wild! (At least in my head).

The next two points went to me, and I somehow managed to win that set despite being ten points back a mere 10 minutes beforehand. I regrouped and got myself back in the zone for the final set. Big breath. At this point, my opponent's mind had gone adrift. He was focused on the negative rumination about how he could have possibly let me come back. Sticking with the plan, I end up winning the final set, and ultimately the tournament.

What followed this particularly enjoyable event were many years of similar experiences. In my athletic career I would have rare moments of intense concentration where I would play *out of my mind.* This was not only limited to sport. There would be moments during amazing conversations or playing a really challenging video game where time seemed to stand still, and I would feel locked into the moment.

Yet I couldn't quite grasp it, and the more I chased the experience the more it seemed to elude me. These optimal states of consciousness fascinated me, and I would later spend a large part of my time trying to understand them more deeply.

My interests eventually steered me towards a book called *The Inner Game of Tennis* by Timothy Gallwey. Even though I wasn't a tennis player, it had some amazing concepts that really spoke to me. In the book, the author talks about athletes playing "out of their mind" where they are not aware of giving themselves a lot of instructions, thinking about how to hit the ball, how to correct past mistakes, and generally just not forcing things. They are conscious, but not thinking, *not over-trying*[7].

We have all experienced something similar, whether knowingly or not, but we may have never fully understood these moments and left them as a mystery. It is time to paint over this elusiveness with the brush of science.

As you will learn, success has no recipe or playbook. But with an open mind and a willingness to explore yourself a little deeper you might get a little closer to improving not only your performance but your overall well-being.

RECAP

- Having no mind is a state of wholeness in which the mind functions freely and easily, without the sensation of a second mind or ego standing over it with a club. It is a Zen term used to describe a feeling of oneness with what you are doing, free from the nagging inner critic.

- We have three basic types of mind:

  1. **Negative** mind (negative self-talk, distraction, unhappy)
  2. **Positive** mind (positive self-talk, focused, happy)
  3. **No mind** (not over-thinking, just doing)

- Another way to describe having a mind without mind, or no mind, is *flow state*. These terms are used interchangeably in this book but refer to the same state of mind where we are free from the thinking self, and instead, move into the doing self.

2

WHAT IS FLOW?

Think back to a moment where you felt and performed at your very best: playing a near-perfect game, shooting 12 for 12, or beating your personal best. It is likely that a flow state is at the root of these moments.

The term *flow* has a weird rep. It tends to be associated with "new age" lifestyle, or spirituality. It is not until recently that the concept of "flow" has resurfaced and been legitimately studied as an aspect of positive psychology and a unique part of the human experience.

When enough people go through a similar experience it starts to enter through the realm of cultural and societal vocabulary. This leads to curious individuals taking note and eventually starting a scientific inquiry. This is what happened with the flow state.

Flow science and research has a rich history dating back around 150 years. Notable philosophers and psychologists such as William James wrote about it as early as the 1800s, and Abraham Maslow who labeled the state *peak experience*[8] starting in the 1940s and '50s. Initially, the study of flow fell under the guise of "mystical experiences", often described in religious scripts such as unity with God, or oneness with the universe. Early on, the flow state was thought to be reserved for spiritual leaders, shamans, or mystics, but as time went on, researchers, thinkers, and philosophers who studied these phenomena noticed that anyone can experience altered states of consciousness such as flow. Thus, we saw a democratization of peak experiences.

The scientific term *flow* emerged from research by the psychologist Mihaly Csikszentmihalyi (pronounced Cheek-sent-me-high) back in the '70s, who conducted one of the most detailed studies on positive human experience[9]. Csikszentmihalyi defined flow as the mental state in which a person performing an activity is fully immersed in a feeling of energized focus, full involvement, and enjoyment in the process of the activity.

You likely have experienced a state of flow while performing your sport. Your ego seems to dissipate, time either slows down, or speeds up, every action, movement, and thought follows inevitably from the previous one, moment by moment. A complete sense of presence.

Michael Jordan recounts a moment of being in this so-called zone:

> *"The crowd gets quiet, and the moment starts to become the moment for me...Once you get into the moment, you know when you are there. Things start to move slowly; you start to see the court very well. You start reading what the defense is trying to do. I saw that moment..."*[10]

In essence, flow is one of the most profound and enjoyable states a human can achieve. It drives human achievement, fosters relationships, and ultimately makes life worthwhile. Flow is an experience of intrinsic motivation in which we feel totally immersed in an activity and perform it for its own sake. It can be also referred to as the "optimal state": those experiencing it report that they are completely involved in an activity to the point of forgetting time, fatigue, and everything else but the activity itself.

Steven Kotler, best selling author of books on flow such as *The Rise of Superman* and *Stealing Fire,* as well as executive director of the Flow Research Collective, defines it as an optimal state of consciousness where we feel our best and we perform at our best[11]. Flow increases our motivation, creativity, learning process, and has been shown to be a primary driver and enhancer of human performance, be it athletic or otherwise.

AN EXPERIENCE WITH MANY NAMES

Some call it *being in the zone;* jazz musicians were said to be *in the pocket;* runners experience a *runner's high.* This optimal state of consciousness has many different names, but whatever you may call it, flow is an altered state where we feel like we're finally in control of the reins. Writers get into a trance-like state—writing pages and pages of a book only to realize a couple of hours later that they haven't stopped to go to the bathroom or even eat. Athletes get out of their own heads and play a near-perfect game.

This euphoric altered state is something you may have experienced in one form or another. Most of us can fathom the idea of flow, what it *feels* like. But when it comes to explaining our experience, we are at a loss for words because words really can't do it justice. It is an experience that transcends vocabulary, time, and space. It is only when we completely tune in to our surroundings, to what is actually in front of us, that we can step into this place called the present moment, or what psychologists call the *elongated now.*

Whatever you call it, flow is the most optimal state a human being can achieve and it has a particular application as we strive to push the boundaries of human performance.

Physical ability has its limitations and the gap in metrics such as strength, speed, and endurance, have been closed to a few inches or milliseconds. But the mind, as far as we know, is limitless. It can push us to greater and higher standards of what is possible. Michael Sachs, a sport psychologist at Temple University has even gone so far as to say that behind every gold medal or world championship that ever been won, there is likely a flow state behind the victory[12].

But what exactly is this elusive state of mind that is behind so many great achievements? Let's take a deeper dive into the science.

THE BRAIN IN FLOW

When we experience flow, we get a sense of stepping out and beyond our-selves, as if we are taken along as passengers by something greater than ourselves. Our inner critic goes silent, we lose our self-consciousness, and we are extremely motivated to continue doing what we are doing.

Contrary to popular belief, when we are in this flow state, we're not using more of our brain to do well, we are actually using less of it. Studies show that parts of our brain deactivate when we perform at our best. To put it in scientific terms, we are experiencing something known as *transient hypofrontality*, first hypothesized by neuroscientist Arne Dietrich[13].

Transient means "for a short period of time." *Hypo* is the opposite of hyper, meaning "low energy." And *frontality* refers to the pre-frontal cortex of the brain which seems to down-regulate (become less active) when experiencing a state of flow.

In flow, our nagging inner critic stops doubting our abilities, and our idea of the self vanishes. Our perception of ourselves is housed within the prefrontal cortex of our brains, alongside other higher cognitive functions. When this goes offline, we no longer see ourselves as a separate entity from our surroundings.

Also located in the prefrontal cortex is our understanding of space and time. This is why in a state of flow our perception of time is skewed: we either feel everything slowed down, (as people report during a car accident for example) or sped up. Many people report not remembering what happened during a peak experience, as if it just flew by. It is likely you don't even remember that perfect game you played last week. It almost seems like a blur.

With the improvement in neuroscience in the last few decades, we are starting to get a clearer picture of what actually happens inside of our brain during altered states of consciousness such as flow. In 2008, Johns Hopkins neuroscientist Charles Limb used functional magnetic resonance imaging (fMRI) to examine the brains of improv jazz musicians in flow[14]. In line with Dietrich's theory of transient hypofrontality, the results showed a down-regulation of the dorsolateral prefrontal cortex which is associated with self-monitoring, self-doubt, and the infamous inner critic. When the dorsolateral prefrontal cortex goes offline, this creates momentum, increased risk-taking, and free-flowing creativity. Thus, jazz musicians in flow are able to improvise and connect musical dots that most musicians don't even see.

Arne Dietrich calls this an *efficiency exchange*: our brain trades the slower and energy-expensive conscious processing usually reserved for higher cognitive functions for faster and more efficient subconscious processing. This is also in line with something called *the dual-process theory of cognition*, which describes the existence of two separate cognitive systems in which humans tend to operate[15]. In this theory, system 1 is the non-conscious, evolutionary old, fast processer while system 2 is the conscious, evolutionarily newer processor capable only of processing a small amount of information in a slower manner. We can think of flow as System 1 *doing* the action[16], while System 2 only gets in the way: a mind without mind!

FLOW & BRAIN CHEMISTRY

Changes in brainwave function also occur in the brain during a state of flow. We see a shift from the fast-moving beta wave patterns of waking consciousness down to the far slower borderline between alpha and theta brain waves. Alpha is known to be our day-dreaming mode, or normal waking consciousness. We shift from idea to idea without much resistance. Theta tends to show up during the rapid eye movement (REM) stage or just before we fall asleep.

The brain's neurochemistry is also changed in flow. Researchers have discovered that endorphins are part of flow with norepinephrine, dopamine, anandamide (your body's version of THC, the psychoactive ingredient found in cannabis), and serotonin showing up consistently. All five are pleasure-inducing, performance-enhancing neurochemicals, upping everything from muscle reaction times to attention, pattern recognition, and lateral thinking[17]. These chemicals are particularly active in the phenomenon known as "runners high", which occurs after a long bout of exercise such as in runners. Although very similar to a state of flow in that they have brain chemistry in common, flow is more of a cognitive state of mind, while runner's high is possibly the body's physiological response to pain in prolonged exercise. Nevertheless, exercise can be a great way to induce similar feelings of euphoria like in flow, in something known as *exercise-induced transient hypofrontality.*

MAKING YOURSELF MORE FLOW PRONE

Flow states currently lack a systematic method of training[18]. It is quite difficult to directly train someone to get into flow. However, by understanding the mechanics behind it we can start to unravel and create the right conditions for flow to emerge more consistently. It is similar to the story of a Zen monk who, when asked by his student how to reach enlightenment, says it pretty much happens by accident. This surprises the student and he becomes angry, wondering why the master put him through so many hours of meditation, tests and exercises to have it all come down to an accident. "Ahh," says the master, "but all this training makes you more accident-prone!."

In the same way, getting into flow is a very fragile task, but there are ways to help get your mind and body more *flow prone*. Many years of study have demonstrated certain patterns that make optimal performance more likely. Mihaly Csikszentmihalyi alongside numerous other researchers revealed four prerequisites (antecedents) to entering flow, as well as six common outcomes that we experience after being in the state. These conditions are considered the gold standard for researching and identifying flow and is the foundation upon which the training methods in this book are presented. While our outcomes of these antecedents and outcomes have since expanded, here are the original conditions for experiencing flow states[19]:

ANTECEDENTS (pre-requisites or requirements to entering a flow state)

1. Focused attention
2. Clear goals
3. A balance between challenge and skill level
4. Unambiguous feedback

PROCESS OUTCOMES (what you experience while in flow)

- Complete concentration in the present moment
- Merging of action and awareness
- Sense of control

- Loss of self-consciousness
- Distortion of time
- Intrinsic motivation

Essentially, flow can only arise when all of our attention is focused in the present moment, so that's what these flow triggers do; they drive attention into the here and now. In other words, these triggers are the very things that evolution shaped our brain to pay the most attention to, so by understanding them, you can use your own psychology and physiology to your advantage. What the research suggests is that without meeting the four necessary conditions, the outcomes associated with the feeling of flow, such as focused attention and distortion of time, is less likely to occur. However, even if prior conditions are met, it is not guaranteed that you will experience each of the six process outcomes of the flow state.

While researching flow in sports, Csikszentmihalyi and Susan Jackson discovered that the flow experience falls on a spectrum[20]. You can be in a state of micro-flow or a lighter version of the state—like what happens when you make a few good shots in a row in basketball. Or you can experience a state of macro-flow, where all of those core characteristics show up all at once—such as losing your perception of space and time during an ultra-endurance race.

Research undertaken by the Flow Research Collective led by Steven Kotler further expand on flow research literature and have found more flow triggers. According to Kotler, there are 17 or more known triggers[21] (though these need more empirical evidence).

Flow can be further broken down into psychological and environmental triggers (as well as social, which I will touch on later) that can help enhance its likelihood. We do not yet fully understand all possible flow triggers, but it seems that the individual experience of flow requires all or at least some of the *psychological conditions* mentioned above (complete concentration, immediate feedback, clear goals, and challenge skill balance), as well as the following *environmental conditions*:

- High consequence (risk)
- Novelty
- Unpredictability
- Complexity
- Deep embodiment
- Pattern recognition

Psychological conditions can be honed by the individual through systematic mental training and can be amplified by certain environmental conditions, that if approached with intention and care, can be a unique recipe for peak experiences. Let's dive a little deeper into each one of the triggers and conditions of flow to get a better understanding.

PSYCHOLOGICAL CONDITIONS FOR FLOW

Challenge-Skill Balance

In 1908, psychologists Robert M. Yerkes and John Dillingham Dodson hypothesized a relationship between performance and anxiety which states that performance increases with physiological or mental arousal, but only up to a certain point. When levels of arousal become too high, performance decreases.

The process is often illustrated graphically as a bell-shaped curve that increases and decreases with higher levels of arousal and is now known as the Yerkes Dodson Law, otherwise known as the *Inverted U Hypothesis*[22]. This was one of the inspirations for Csikszentmihalyi's research on flow. He found a similar relationship for experiencing peak performance, where having the right balance between your skill level and the perceived level of demand for any given activity is crucial to creating ripe conditions for flow.

Essentially, flow is more likely to occur when we feel just the right amount of challenge compared to our perceived level of skill. Compared to other conditions, challenge–skill balance is one of the most robust contributors to flow[23]. If you perceive the challenge to be too high, and your skill level to be low, you can get overwhelmed and anxious. If skill exceeds the challenge, then you get bored and do not grow. The key is to find an activity that provides just the right amount of challenge that you are pushed to step outside your comfort level. This is illustrated in the following graph:

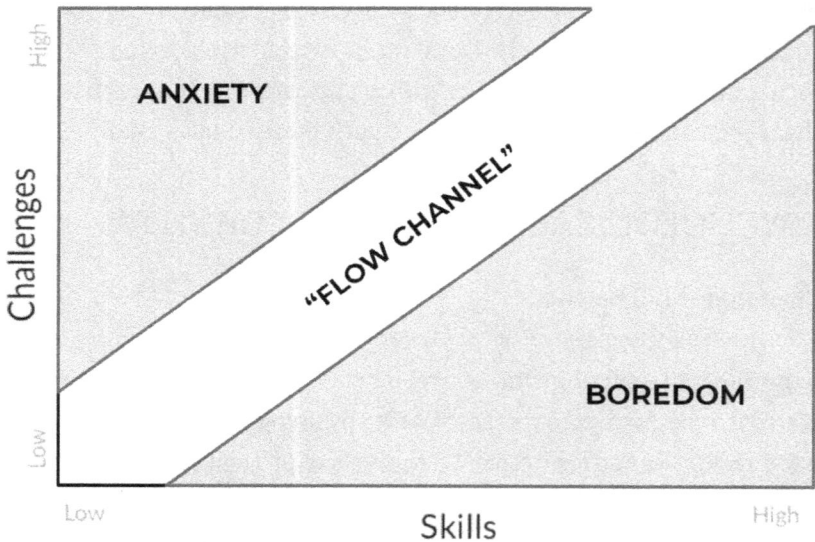

People differ in the extent to which challenges and skills are related to each other. Some research suggests that in activities we perceive as unimportant and as having no important consequences, a totally equal balance between difficulty and skill should lead to flow experiences[24]. On the other hand, if you consider the task to be important to you with important consequences, then you tend to only experience flow when your skill exceeds the difficulty of the task. The explanation for this is that in activities that we perceive as having highly important consequences, the threat of potential failure will hinder the experience of flow. However, if your skill is higher than the challenge requires, you feel more comfortable and are more likely to have a flow experience.

In a general sense, flow can be achieved at varying stages of perceived challenge and skill but is stronger as you move up the graph. This explains why you may experience micro-flow in situations such as having a conversation with a friend, but a seasoned rock climber will experience a greater thrill from ascending a 5.15 D cliff[25]. The rock climber has more at stake and the challenge is more difficult.

Personality seems to also be a factor that adds to the complexity of the challenge-skill balance. Csikszentmihalyi found that people with a personality catered towards high achievement, something he called an *autotelic personality*, would naturally seek activities with more challenge. Individuals that are high achievers tend to experience flow more frequently than low achievers[26]. Thus, it goes without saying that sitting on your couch watching skiing videos will not put you in as grand a flow state as you would if you were actually skiing.

The 4% Rule

There is some debate over whether skill must perfectly match the demands of the challenge, or if flow is greater when challenge exceeds perceived ability. Csikszentmihalyi himself went back and forth on this. Some of his studies showed the ratio of challenges to skill should be around 50/50 for an optimal experience, with even a slight imbalance causing anxiety. On the other hand, a study done on chess players revealed that their levels of enjoyment were the highest when playing against an opponent who was better, compared to an equally ranked opponent. In this case, when perceived challenges were higher than the perceived skill level, the players enjoyed the games more[27].

It is tough to say what the ideal ratio is, as many factors come into play. After all, this is *perceived* challenge and skill, so people vary in the extent to which one's skills and the perception of challenges are related. Perhaps some people just have a greater tolerance to an imbalance and greater challenge demands. However, it must be taken into consideration that the whole point of learning any activity is to get better. Being perfectly balanced in the demands of the challenge might be pleasurable for the time being, but eventually, you need to challenge yourself in order to push the boundaries of what's possible and grow as a performer.

Learning is not a linear process and keeping your challenge just above your skill level will ensure that you promote the process of skill acquisition and learning. Of course, this is difficult to master, as too much challenge will leave you feeling overwhelmed. With practice, however, you can decipher what the range is in which you can learn to play. Most people have a range of tolerance where the demands don't necessarily diminish performance gains. It varies from person to person, but a good rule of thumb to consider is having challenge around 4% higher than skill. This is an arbitrary number and is difficult to measure, so take it with a grain of salt. However, it can help map out your performance demands and guide you towards growth and mastery. Basically, you want to stretch, not snap.

4% does not seem like much, but it has a cumulative effect over time as increasing the challenge just a small percentage at a time daily, weekly, or monthly will eventually increase your competence. As a result, you will find yourself slowly moving up in skill and into greater and greater potentialities of experiencing macro levels of flow. This is why the highest level of any sporting competition or activity will produce the most exciting yet anxious moments. As the legendary soccer player Pelé says: "the more difficult the victory, the greater the happiness in winning."

This is what we call the razor's edge of performance, or the upper limits of one's own potential. What does 4% feel like? That is very much up to the individual. A 4% increase in one person can equate to a 10% increase in challenge for someone else resulting in feelings of anxiousness. It isn't meant to be a perfect calculation but rather a guide in ensuring that you are constantly pushing the upper limits of what is possible for you.

Immediate/Unambiguous feedback

Feedback is the process of providing performers with frequent and accurate measures against a known standard of performance. In the absence of adequate feedback, even highly motivated people will struggle with efficient learning, and will only see minimal improvement. We need to know exactly how we're doing in order to have an accurate representation of our performance. Too often we go about our craft with no clear idea if what we are doing is correct or not. With feedback, we are better able to adjust, and course-correct our technique, work, performance, etc.

The research is clear that feedback has to be immediate and unambiguous. This means there needs to be a reduced time gap for feedback between our input (our efforts) and output (the result of what we put in). If feedback is not immediate, we start to look for things we've done in the past, or compare ourselves to others, both of which pull us out of the present moment.

Coaches and managers can improve on this by providing more frequent and clear feedback to their athletes. Keeping the feedback loops tight is an effective way of making sure everyone is on the same page and reduces role ambiguity. The more someone understands what their role is and gets consistent adequate feedback, the better their performance will be, and if enough individuals on a team feel this way, the group itself is more likely to tap into group flow (which I will discuss later).

Clear Objectives/Goals

We all know the cliche saying: you cannot hit a target you cannot see. But there is something that rings true in this. When you were a child first learning to walk, there was usually a very clear target. Your parents were calling your name, usually enticing you with some food or a toy to play with. The goal was the thing that helped you find any means necessary to get there quicker. It channeled your focus and lined up a series of steps. Literally. When the objective is clear, it clarifies our thoughts and actions.

But this only works when our goals are *process*-oriented, rather than *outcome*-oriented. Focusing our attention on the outcome ironically worsens our chances of reaching it. This is because in an outcome (also called ego) goal orientation, the focus is on social comparison to judge personal ability and competence. The outcome-oriented person's primary source of motivation is being better than others. On the contrary, the process-oriented (also known as task or mastery) focus is on self-improvement, effort, and personal mastery to judge personal ability and competence. Imagine focusing on your personal best rather than on besting an opponent. In this way, your perceived ability is not tied solely to your success.

One of the dominant theories in motivation, Achievement Goal Theory (AGT), proposes that people who focus on task goals are more resilient to nagging doubts and criticism regardless of perceived competence. This is because they do not need to be better than others to feel good about themselves[28]. Another reason why you should focus on the process is that the outcome of any given event or situation is never 100% fully in your control. So, it doesn't make sense to set goals like winning a championship or being the best in your field without first addressing the elements—the skills that you have as an individual—that directly impact the outcome.

Setting clear goals means outlining the micro-steps that channel your attention to what needs to be done *right now.* Do you want to make the University soccer team? Great! But how many other players are out there competing for your spot? Can you control how well they do? Can you control whether or not the coaches decide to pick you for their squad? Sure, there are things you can do to increase your chances of getting selected, but ultimately it is the coach who decides, not you. Why then, should you spend so much cognitive and physical energy on things you have little control over? Instead, you should be focusing on clear micro goals on which you actually have an impact, such as increasing your own skills, stamina, and understanding of your personal performance to be as good as an athlete as you can be. The more you are clear on what you need to do next to meet your short-term goals, the more momentum you gather to ultimately reach your long-term goals.

I always get a kick out of runners who spend so much time figuring out what splits they will run for a competition, focusing on each millisecond. But why over complicate it? You've already put in all the work training for this event, so trust yourself and just run! If you show up mentally and physically you will be able to take in all the things thrown at you, including the inevitable setbacks.

The more we are receptive to the moment—malleable and without attachment—the greater likelihood of achieving our goals. Understand that there is no such thing as a perfect performance. There is only the presence of mind to be in the moment and to enjoy the process. With this kind of mindset, you are more likely to achieve the results that you want.

Focused Attention

How often do you find yourself telling yourself or someone else that you just don't have the time? We've all been there. We would rather be watching our favourite show, than going out for a run or working on writing a book (guilty as charged). But the reality is not that you don't have time to do what you want (workout, socialize, study, etc.), it's because you haven't trained yourself to manage your time appropriately. Top performers make the most of their time, and the way they maximize their time is to increase their focus. Let go of all distractions and just focus on what you need to do. That is true focus.

Focus isn't the attention itself, but rather the tuning out of everything that is unnecessary to the task at hand. If a tennis player needs to serve, focusing on the crowd or how good their opponent is just isn't relevant to the task. The athlete needs to let go of the external stimuli which serve no purpose to hitting an ace.

Will we get distracted from time to time? Of course! But the key is to catch yourself in these moments when you get distracted and bring that attention back to the goal. It is not focus itself, but rather bringing the attention back when the mind has wandered. Focused attention and clear objectives/goals are closely intertwined in this sense, because we must constantly bring our attention to the goal, which can either be at the macro-level of focus (such as big goals and plans like winning a championship), or at the micro-level (such as acing a serve). Keeping our focus on the task at hand creates ripe conditions for flow state and is something that must be constantly trained.

Without sustained focus, we are prone to dysfunctional performance. Thus, it is crucial to have just the right amount of focus. The ideal space is what practitioners of Zen call an *effortless effort*: holding your focus loosely but with the right intention. With consistent practice, you too can train your mind to focus on the right things when it matters the most.

ENVIRONMENTAL CONDITIONS FOR FLOW

Once we have mastered the psychological conditions for flow, we can look to the environment to aid in increasing our ability to get out of our own head and into flow. High-performance environments are ripe with various uncontrollable conditions that, if properly understood and harnessed, can be a recipe for rapt concentration and presence of mind. You might be expecting something very complex, but these conditions are fairly simple, and the variables can be easily manipulated. Let's take a look at how we can use certain environmental factors as triggers for flow.

High Consequences (Risk)

Risk is a potent flow trigger. It heightens our awareness and drop kicks us into the present moment almost instantaneously. If you have ever stood over a tall building looking down at the abyss below, I would bet you weren't thinking about what you had for lunch that day. This is why extreme sports athletes tend to experience flow more often, since there is a high degree of risk involved. Jumping off a cliff, or free solo climbing a mountain, or any extreme sport with high stakes, comes with a lot of physical risk. Risk has been shown to ignite our fear response, which narrows our focus and heightens our awareness, thus increasing the likelihood of a flow state. Of course, I am not telling you to put yourself in harm's way, but rather find just the right amount of risk to increase your focus (think back to the 4% rule).

For example, I like to go for trial runs. However, I sometimes misjudge the conditions. One particular winter day, I was dealing with some slippery and icy terrain and found myself in a pretty risky situation. There were some steep inclines on this trail, that I could have slipped and fallen down if I wasn't careful, hurting myself in the process. But I took up this unanticipated challenge and found myself with a heightened sense of awareness and focus. This high-risk situation came with a high reward as I dove into a flow state weaving my way through the trails. This is because we are wired to focus on whatever is in front of us whenever we feel any threat. This was an adaptive strategy for our ancestors who ran from predators on a daily basis. Being distracted while being chased by a tiger is a sure way to make sure you come out on the losing end.

However, risk doesn't only come in the form of physical harm. It can be social risk, such as leaving your current team for another, or a financial risk such as leaving your job to pursue an Olympic dream. Risks can also be emotional, spiritual, or intellectual. Depending on your tolerance for each type, these are all potential triggers for heightened awareness and focus, and when used appropriately, can be a very potent way to increase performance.

Human progress was never made by avoiding the things that scare us. Think of all the achievements that would have went undone without risk: the Wright brothers never successfully flying the first airplane, or Copernicus being too afraid to question the dominant model of the Earth being at the center of the universe—no risk, no reward.

Rich Environment

This means an environment that is rich with novelty, unpredictability, and complexity. Novelty means surrounding yourself with something new, which will catch and keep your attention. Our brains are wired for novelty. This is why any time you travel somewhere new, you feel excited about every new thing you see. This is dopamine in action, and our brain loves new stimuli. Whenever we get a hit of dopamine in our system, we are more likely to pay attention to what we're doing, and thus our learning effectiveness tends to increase. To apply novelty, you can practice new skills, or train in a completely new environment to spice things up. For example, workout in a new gym every once in a while or shoot some hoops on a completely different court.

Rich environments are also filled with unpredictability and complexity. This means that when you're in one, you're stepping outside your comfort zone and facing the unknown; you're also increasing the depth and breadth of your knowledge by seeking out information from many different sources or viewpoints.

As I mentioned above, I like to incorporate new rich environments filled with novelty and unpredictability during my runs. This means choosing new and unfamiliar routes, running in different weather, or at different times during the day. Rich environments are also a big creativity trigger, so they can help establish new neural pathways and connections that might have not been there previously.

Deep Embodiment

This trigger involves incorporating the entire body in space. Far too often we go about our daily activities very one-dimensionally without noticing our entire bodily experience. Paying attention to multiple sensory streams at once can bring us into a full-body experience. Taking the time to really tune into your surroundings will drive attention to the present.

Next time you are out on a run, on the court, or the field, see if you can notice and pay attention to all the different senses: notice all the different colours, and listen to each distinct sound you hear, for instance. Bringing your whole body into the experience can really make you feel as if there is no separation between the two. For example, during a break in play, a hockey player can notice the temperature at the rink, the feeling of her skates on the ice, and the smell of popcorn from the concession.

Deep embodiment can also be considered an outcome of flow state as we tend to feel more in tune with our environment. It begins by paying attention to the various input and stimuli that surround us.

This is why humans tend to learn the best kinesthetically (by doing), rather than just by visual or auditory stimuli. Since all our senses are involved in the process of learning by doing, if we're just listening to instruction without doing the action, our minds may wander. Some sports are naturally better for deep embodiment, such as gymnastics, skate/snowboarding, and skiing. In these sports, the individual moves the body in multiple dimensions and must always be in tune with their center of gravity, which helps the athlete achieve embodiment.

Pattern Recognition

Humans are wired for recognizing patterns and things that are familiar. We start to make sense of novel and complex environments by focusing on what already works. Ideas don't just come out of the blue. Previous patterns must link together, which can then spark creative ideas. This becomes a flow trigger: when we link old and new ideas together, we get a boost in neurochemicals like norepinephrine and dopamine which enhance our attention so that we may continue to detect more patterns[29].

An athlete can use pattern recognition by linking similar training scenarios with in-game ones. For example, a soccer player can practice free kicks in various positions and with opponents in the wall. Then, once the player is in a similar spot during a game, the player's brain will recognize a pattern has emerged, since they've seen it before. Thus, they are more likely to execute the action effectively.

The mental skill of imagery, or visualization is a great way to practice pattern recognition. By imagining situations, events, and patterns in your mind's eye prior to an event, you can help drive the mind and body connection. The reason imagery works like this is because the same neurological pathways are activated when we visualize doing an activity, as when we do the activity for real.

HOW DO I KNOW IF I AM IN FLOW?

Once we have the right psychological and environmental conditions set, certain things tend to occur. Years of psychological research have created a list of commonly mentioned experiences of flow which we will go over in detail next. An individual can experience all, or some of these in no particular order.

Merging of Action and Awareness

In flow, there is no separation between your thoughts and your actions. They both seem to move seamlessly and fluidly from one moment to the next without interruption. The thinking mind seems to shut down and doesn't get in the way of the actual doing.

Timothy Gallwey, author of *The Inner Game of Tennis*, describes this as a battle between Self One, or the thinking self, and Self Two, the doing self. This is similar to the dual-process theory of cognition that I mentioned earlier (System 1 versus System 2). Once we learn to get Self One out of the way, Self Two can just focus on performing. For example, a tennis player focuses on the *feeling* of the ball hitting the racquet and does not judge each swing as good or bad. He keeps his attention on the action and the sensation, rather than on judgment or scorekeeping.

Often, those who have experienced flow mention it as if they are just a casual observer to what is happening. Athletes may talk about flow as if their every movement or action was on autopilot, or like someone else was pulling the strings.

It isn't that someone else is doing the action for us, but rather there is no longer a separation of self and the awareness of there being a self in the first place. This is primarily where the term "flow" originates, as people would describe their experiences of action-awareness merging as being fluid, as if they were flowing through an activity, almost like water.

Sense of Control

Because of the blending of action and awareness in flow, we tend to experience a sense of complete control over our activity when in this flow state. A snowboarder, for example, can feel as if they are in sync with the board and can finely manipulate and carve their way through deep snow with ease. Ironically, we do not gain control by forcing things to happen but by giving into the experience itself. Although it seems like we are in full control in flow, we may also feel as if it is not us performing the action. Some psychologists call this the Paradox of Control. The snowboarder may feel like the board is riding him, not the other way around.

Dr. Dylan Taylor, a cardiologist at the Mazankowski Heart Institute in Alberta, Canada, describes the feeling of flow in the operating room as a symphony between the task at hand and the surgery itself. Dr. Taylor becomes completely immersed with each action and embodies complete precision and the feeling of being in control. Speed, in this case, can quite literally kill, so he must slow things down. As he puts it; "slow is smooth, and smooth is fast." There is no need to rush because the act takes care of itself if he just gets out of his own way[30]. The more he tries to control each movement, the tighter he will become. Thus, by giving away the control, the surgery seems to happen on its own.

Loss of Self-Consciousness

Inside flow there is no room for self-doubt or for a heightened awareness of the self. It wastes too much cognitive energy. The quieting of the pre-frontal cortex common in flow states creates a quieting of self-consciousness; the brain is conducting an energy efficiency exchange and too much focus on self takes too much energy.

Self-analysis and self-consciousness are housed in the pre-frontal cortex. Since this area tends to go offline during flow states, we no longer worry about how we look or the consequences of a particular action; worrying is not conducive to the task at hand. By saving cognitive energy on not worrying about *who* the "actor" is, we can focus more on the *act itself*. As one can imagine, it can be quite pleasurable to turn down the volume on self-analysis.

Some neuroscientists are playing around with the idea of artificially inducing this loss of self. Sally Adee, a science and technology writer, experienced this loss of self firsthand when conducting field research for an article. She was given transcranial direct current stimulation, or tDCS for short (a mild electrical current sent through the brain) in order to quiet her pre-frontal cortex. She was then put through an accelerated marksmanship training, a training simulation that the military uses, learning how to shoot a modified M4 close-range assault rifle. Sally describes the experiences as such:

> *"...what defined the experience was not feeling smarter or learning faster: the thing that made the earth drop out from under my feet was that for the first time in my life, everything in my head finally shut up... my brain without self-doubt was a revelation."*[31]

The absence of self-preoccupation allows us to shift our focus to the task at hand while rejecting extraneous and egocentric distractions. We could all do with a little more quiet upstairs, don't you think?

Distortion of Time

In addition to self-consciousness, time is also perceived in the pre-frontal cortex. During hypofrontality we get the sense of time either speeding up or slowing down. Just like with self-consciousness, it is an efficiency exchange. Basically, our brain figures out it needs a lot of energy for focusing attention, so it pulls energy away from non-critical areas such as keeping track of the future and the past. Since most of our fears are either in the past or in the future, we get obvious benefits from not being stuck in rumination.

Therefore, in flow we may experience either time slowing down or speeding up.

A gamer in a state of flow can be up all night and can come out of it and not know what time it is, feeling as if it was only an instant. On the other hand, a difficult and closely contested match can feel like an eternity. However, the reason why we experience speeding up or a slowing down effect remains unclear. It may be that when you are in a stressful situation, slowing things down is our brain's adaptive strategy for self-preservation.

Intrinsic Motivation (Autotelic Experience)

When it comes to motivation, there are two basic types: *extrinsic motivation* and *intrinsic motivation. Extrinsic* motivation is being motivated to do something by something external to you, such as money, fame, or being forced to do it, such as sticking with a particular sport because your parents wish it. *Intrinsic motivation,* on the other hand, is doing something because it is inherently valuable to you: you enjoy the experience of it and don't require any external influence. Research shows that individuals with more intrinsic motivation tend to stick with activities for the long term and find more joy out of the experience. With flow, the experience is intrinsic: it's the experience itself that keeps us coming back for more. It is rewarding in and of itself.

Csikszentmihalyi found that some people are more prone to being intrinsically motivated and labeled this type of personality as *autotelic*, from the Greek words *autos* (self) and *telos* (goal). Individuals with an autotelic personality tend to be high achievers and naturally seek tasks with more challenge. The mark of the autotelic personality, Csikszentmihalyi says, is the ability to manage a rewarding balance between the 'play' of challenge finding, and the 'work' of skill-building. Csikszentmihalyi writes:

"An autotelic person needs few material possessions and little entertainment, comfort, power, or fame because so much of what he or she does is already rewarding. Because such person's experience flow in work, in family life, when interacting with people, when eating, even when alone with nothing to do, they depend less on external rewards that keep others motivated to go on with a life of routines. They are more autonomous and independent because they cannot be as easily manipulated with threats or rewards from the outside. At the same time, they are more involved with everything around them because they are fully immersed in the current of life."[32]

Autotelic involvement is characterized by feelings of personal whole-ness, a sense of discovery, and a sense of human connectedness. Athletes who are more intrinsically motivated are more likely to enjoy their sport since they do it for the pure satisfaction of doing the activity. Many athletes lose the passion that once drove the pursuit of their craft once the external rewards of money become a contributing factor. As such, their performance tends to decline, or their careers don't last very long. I'll discuss how to manage this tendency in part three of this book.

THE BENEFITS OF FLOW

Flow is highly desirable for athletes because of its relationship with peak performance. Interestingly, we experience more joy out of activities that are challenging and require skill (such as sports!) compared to passive activities such as watching television. In fact, one study showed that when compared to rock climbing, test subjects who spend more time sitting at home experienced twice as much anxiety, and fewer occasions for flow[33].

35

Flow is also particularly relevant to the elite cohort of athletes or other performers for whom margins between success and failure tend to be very small, such as milliseconds of time, or inches of space. In flow, we think our best, we feel our best, and we perform at our best[34].

However, and possibly more importantly, there is also a large body of scientific evidence that indicates flow is highly correlated with happiness in the long term. There is a range of psychological benefits such as enhanced well-being and a healthier concept of self that are related to flow[35].

Across lifespans, the pursuit of happiness has become a priority for most, if not all individuals. Flow plays a vital role in this endeavor. Many studies confirm that experiencing flow is an important predictor of subjective emotional well-being and of healthy aging[36]. Flow also strongly correlates with learning; any activity we engage in with high enjoyment, motivation, and concentration can facilitate the subjective experience of flow and can help us learn[37].

How to create flow states and instill intrinsic motivation to pursue life's challenges is at the core of what it means to be human. We all desire optimal experiences, whether through athletic performance, relationships, or whatever journey one pursues. Thus, promoting and training your mind to experience the precursors to the flow state can contribute to a life filled with pleasurable and meaningful experiences.

WHY IS FLOW IMPORTANT?

When looking at the most important motivational factors for motivation, humans need to fulfill three basic needs: to feel like they belong, to feel competent, and to have the autonomy to make choices. This is the premise behind self-determination theory, a macro theory of human motivation and personality[38].

Research has suggested that whenever people experience an environment that supports autonomy, they experience a greater quality of motivation[39]. To put it simply, we naturally gravitate towards things that we have control over, we feel competent in, and that make us feel like we are part of something bigger.

Self-determination is important for us to experience flow in any aspect of life. For example, we know from research that individuals who are physically active for a long period of time seem to prioritize enjoyment and revitalization more than exercising for appearance and weight management[40]. In other words, pursuing activities that are naturally enjoyable and meaningful to us will produce the most flow and we are more likely to continue doing them. If more organizations, teams, and even societies dedicated themselves to developing the right conditions for flow to naturally occur, then I believe the potential would expand not only for human performance but also for our capacity to fulfill our self-actualization needs.

Flow in itself is intrinsically motivating, which means we do an activity purely for the joy it brings us. This naturally brings us to a state of well-being. However, if we were to say that motivation simply comes from the strong will of a particular individual, we would be looking at the issue very one-dimensionally. Many factors such as social inequality, environmental factors, genetic susceptibility, and learned helplessness play huge roles in how we think and behave, including in how we experience or pursue the precursors to flow.

What might be a positive experience for one person in terms of staying active, for example, could be negative for another person because of a past experience that caused this person to view physical activity as something at which they are inadequate (for example, a bad physical education teacher). It is necessary then, that we seek to understand what it is that puts us into flow most often and learn to train ourselves accordingly in order to experience life at its fullest potential.

The more researchers, sport psychologists, coaches, and athletes are able to understand and explain flow, the greater the chance we have of enhancing our performance and experience within sport and life to the highest levels possible. Flow is what creates the possibility for a mind without mind, and in many ways, a life worth living. What we are seeking is not necessarily peace of mind, but rather peace *from* our minds. Flow allows us to end the ceaseless inner chatter which creates a greater potential for happiness and peak performance.

LEARN TO SURRENDER

This is great and all, you might be thinking, but how do I actually get into flow? After all, theory without application isn't going to get you anywhere. The point of this book wasn't to bore you with psychological jargon and to impress you with fancy terms like transient hypofrontality (well, maybe a little bit...). What I really want is to help you achieve a greater sense of purpose and understanding, as well as teach you some tangible techniques to get you out of your own way and create a state of no mind.

However, as of yet, there is no magic button to press that will drop you into an altered state of high performance. As it is with any path to mastery and success, there is no step-by-step process to get into flow. The only thing we can do is develop the right skills and tweak the right conditions so that we can make ourselves more *flow prone*. The good news though, is that we can stack the odds in our favour through conditioning our minds with systematic mental training. All that is required is that you are willing to put the work in and set up the right psychological, environmental, and social conditions so that you can access a greater sense of presence, well-being, and elevated performance more often.

Although many of us might have experienced flow, most of us have a vague understanding of what it actually is, and as such, lack the proper vocabulary. Flow experiences are some of the least understood phenomena in sport. Though the last few decades have shown us some interesting information about decoding peak human performance, the mechanisms behind achieving the flow state are still in their infancy.

But this does not mean we can't go out and experiment with it ourselves. The potential for deciphering the role that psychological, physical, social, and environmental factors play in setting the stage for the optimal state is something that can push individuals and teams towards greater potentialities. How then can you train your mind to reach optimal performance and well-being?

Most likely, you already have the physical and technical ability to perform. But something brought you to read this book. I am here to argue that all the discipline and work ethic you have put in up to this point has not been enough. However, I'm not suggesting putting in *more* work, but rather quite the opposite. All that you have is already inside you. You just need to get out of your own way and let it happen.

But don't misinterpret my words. This is not some new-age spiritual mantra where we just simply "go with the flow" and see what happens. Let's make this clear: one does not experience flow by simply surrendering to the moment. We must have a concentrated and deliberate focus on what we are doing. We must attack the present moment with ferocity. Being the warrior that you are, I am sure you have that intensity about you. I am not here to question that. What is required for you is to relinquish your obsession with the outcome of what may happen. This is what holds most performers back. They just can't trust their body to do the work for them. Therefore, in addition to discipline, there must be an element of surrender in order to reach flow state.

DISCIPLINE   FLOW   SURRENDER

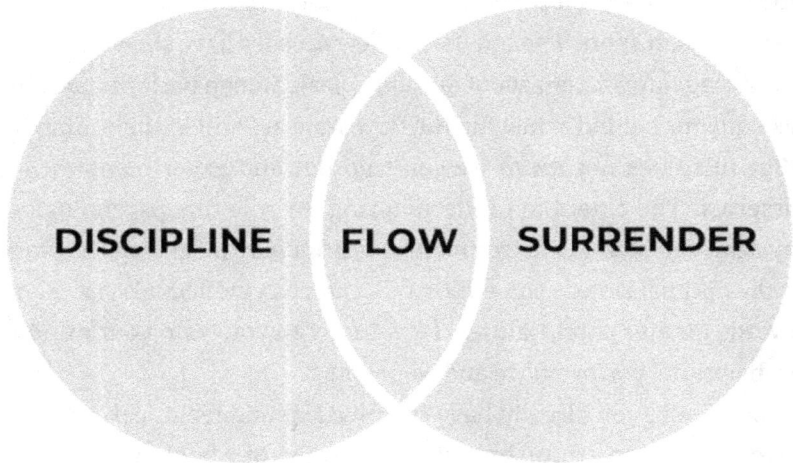

Most individuals I have worked with already come to our work with a great deal of discipline. They are high performers after all, and wouldn't have gotten to that level by slacking on the necessary work. But the most common trait they all share is their ability to trust their training and to simply *let things happen.*

Unless you are a beginner at something, chances are you have put in a sufficient number of hours training your particular craft. Therefore, the neurological adaptations of skill acquisition are already integrated into your brain. There will always be things we can improve from a technical standpoint of course, but in most cases with highly trained performers, when we aren't seeing the results we want, we simply lack the trust to get the job done. Our overthinking self gets in the way!

BE WATER, MY FRIEND

When you first learned to walk as a toddler, you probably failed many times. Actually, let's be honest, you failed a lot. You got a few steps in, and then fell, over and over again. Quite embarrassing actually. But at no point when you fell did you likely think to yourself, *this is not for me!* and gave up. There was a surrendering to the process (albeit unconsciously at this point) and you diligently tried and tried again until you got it right.

Discipline without surrender is just ego. It is an unwinnable game that taunts you with the idea that doing more will bring you success. Take for example a lesson from nature, in particular the flow of water. When water is faced with an unmovable object such as a rock, it doesn't try and go through it with force, but rather it finds its way around it. Without effort, it continues on its path. Actor and martial artist Bruce Lee understood this very well:

> *"Empty your mind, be formless, shapeless — like water. Now you put water in a cup, it becomes the cup; You put water into a bottle it becomes the bottle; You put it in a teapot it becomes the teapot. Now water can flow or it can crash. Be water, my friend."*

The right amount of each characteristic of discipline and surrender varies for each person, but there are trainable components to each. This is where mental skills training plays a huge role in preparing for the journey of high performance. Before you begin a deeper understanding of flow, you must first develop necessary foundational mental skills that will ensure your ability to bounce back from setbacks, as well as to avoid some of the hidden traps that come with pursuing excellence (more on this in part three).

The mental skills such as confidence, grit, resiliency, and optimism are but a few of the foundational pieces that can move you towards peak performance. Taking on any difficult task is challenging and there will be moments of doubt and even failure. The Navy SEALs have a way of dealing with this. They understand that the world is VUCA: volatile, uncertain, complex, and ambiguous, but they learn to *embrace the suck.*

Things are going to get tough out there, but that doesn't mean it's not worth the struggle.

When we shift our perspective from trying to avoid pain, embarrassment, or failure, to seeing all of the above as a necessary part of the process, we can really begin to elevate our game. Developing mental skills such as grit and perseverance will teach you to embrace the suck when the going gets tough and stay on track towards your goals. Once you master these psychological skills and habits, you are better able to move into states of flow.

RECAP

Flow is an optimal state of consciousness where we feel our best, and we perform at our best. In flow we may experience all or some of the following:

1. Complete concentration
2. A sense of control
3. Altered perception of time (slowed down or sped up)
4. Loss of self-consciousness
5. The merging of action and awareness
6. Intrinsic motivation

To experience flow state, some of the following psychological conditions must be met:

- A balance between one's skill level, and the perceived challenge of the activity
- Clear objectives
- Unambiguous and immediate feedback

- Focused attention (deep focus)

In addition to psychological triggers, our environment can play a big role in how we experience flow. It is up to us to manipulate certain conditions to optimize our flow. Some of these environmental triggers are:

- Deep embodiment
- High risk/consequences
- Novelty
- Pattern recognition

We can simplify the triggers and outcomes of flow with the acronym STER:

- **S**elflessness
- **T**imelessness
- **E**ffortlessness
- Information **R**ichness

Currently, there is no systematic method of training for flow. However, we can increase our susceptibility to flow through understanding and applying the various triggers.

II

PART TWO: TRAINING FOR FLOW

"You must unlearn, what you have learned."

– Yoda

3

THE ROAD TO MENTAL MASTERY

In part two, I will introduce the Mental Performance Training (MPT) model in which I have applied to my own life, as well as used to condition the individuals I have worked with. It encompasses the foundational mental skills of self-awareness, confidence, goal setting, and resiliency while training the right conditions for flow state. With the application of this model, I have found consistent decreases in performance barriers such as performance anxiety, lack of confidence and focus, as well as an increase in the frequency of flow state. These were measured through various metrics used pre-and post-intervention. While of course these results are subjective, anyone would agree that a feeling of reduced burden of anxiety, lack of confidence, focus, etc. would most certainly improve performance, or at the very least an increased sense of well-being. That being said, the work really all comes down to the reader. The more you make mental training a priority in your life the more you start to take control. It is recommended that you follow each stage in order as they build upon one another in sequence. This training model is not only intended to improve sports performance but also master the performance of life itself. You will find that the skills can be applied to many domains, with the ultimate philosophy being *individual first* and *performer second.*

Part one sought to understand the *what* and the *why* of training a mind without mind, otherwise known as flow state. Having a strong knowledge of the architecture behind our minds is the first step towards refining the tools to help it grow, and one cannot use the tools without sharpening them first.

Part two then is all about the *how*. It is intended to give you hands-on, applicable instruments in which to play your favourite metaphorical symphony. This next section introduces a framework for mental training. It's nothing complicated, just a framework upon which you can start the process of formally conditioning the mind for the challenges of life and performance.

TIME TO PUT IN THE WORK!

On the road to mastery, there are only two mistakes: not starting, and not going all the way.

If you have come this far, I assume you are committed to working on your craft. But these are just words on paper. The real work begins with you, out there, on the field, the court, rink, or wherever your battleground may be. This section is dedicated to the tangible, real-world things you can implement into your training.

With the right framework and mental model, we can put the right pieces in play to structure a performance geared towards fulfillment and success, whatever that means to you. As discussed previously, decades of research have provided us with great insights into the requirements and conditions for flow state, and ultimately experiencing the sensation of having a mind without mind.

In the following chapters, you will begin the process of Mental Performance Training (MPT). It is a framework for cognitive training for peak performance that specifically considers enhancing the conditions for flow state. Of course, some conditions require environmental or social triggers which require variables sometimes out of your control. Nevertheless, there are certainly elements in a performance that are controllable and more importantly, trainable.

CONTROL THE CONTROLLABLE

According to high-performance psychologist Michael Gervais, there are fundamentally only three things within our control: our thoughts, attitude, and actions[41]. Although we have little control over what thoughts arise in our mind (more on this in the Mindfulness chapter), we do have full control over which ones to attend to and which thoughts to ignore. This leads to a certain attitude and feeling which results in a certain effort and action. Most athletes would agree that how we think and feel affects the way we perform, so it makes sense to train the conditions that allow us to think, feel, and perform at our best.

Early on in my career as a soccer player, I unfortunately did not grasp the importance of mental training. I wasted so much cognitive energy trying to control everything, usually ending up with little success. For example, I remember a specific moment where I wasn't getting the playing time that I wanted or thought I deserved. This led to consistent feelings of anger and frustration towards my coach. Naturally, this didn't help me get more time on the field. Eventually, during one particular practice I came to the realization that I couldn't control how much playing time I got. At the end of the day, it was the coach that decided who got to play and who did not, so I shifted my attention to myself and focused on having one good practice at a time.

As time went on, I began to perform much better since my attention was solely focused on improving myself and not wasted on trying to change the negatively perceived situation. With this renewed sense of focus, I eventually got the playing time that I wanted. This was my first insight into the power of channeling my focus in the right way; on the things that I have control over.

We must be conscious of where our precious attention and energy are allocated. Reflect on your own situation: Are you wasting time trying to control things you can do little about? Understanding what is and is not within your control is at the core of Mental Performance Training (MPT). It is a common thread that binds all the skills together and we must firmly understand it in order to make the gains we want.

From time to time, you will find yourself in a slump or some sort of setback. It is in these moments that you must remind yourself of the controllables. Energy flows where attention goes, so make sure you are not wasting yours.

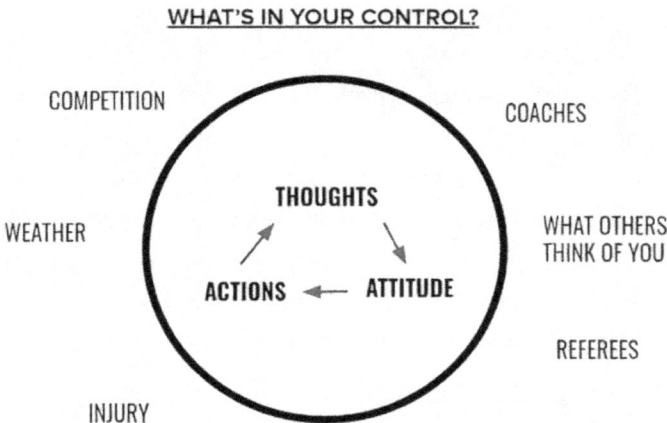

WHAT'S IN YOUR CONTROL?

COMPETITION   COACHES

THOUGHTS

WEATHER   WHAT OTHERS
                                           THINK OF YOU

ACTIONS ←— ATTITUDE

                                              REFEREES

INJURY

CELEBRATE SMALL GAINS

Entering the world of mental training can be different than physical training, where the objective results are easy to measure; mental results can be slower to come to fruition and harder to measure. But in the long run, with a dedication to the mastery of this training, you will see positive results in not only your physical goals but the rest of your life as well.

This doesn't mean you should get discouraged, though; anything worth having takes time. Consider *marginal gains*, a fancy term for tiny improvements over time. No one can make drastic improvements overnight, but rather the slow accumulation of learned technique, behaviour, and habits eventually contributes to the end result. When we look too far into the future or focus on only the end product itself, we can easily get discouraged. But when we view our efforts through a different lens and add some perspective, we can see the results start to add up. James Clear, best selling author of *Atomic Habits*[42], illustrates this point with this principle:

$$1^{365} = 1$$
$$(1.01)^{365} = 37.8$$
$$(0.99)^{365} = 0.03$$

Clear calls habit the compound interest of self-improvement. If you just improve one percent each day for one year, you'll end up thirty-seven times better by the time you're done (1% increase from 1, raised to the power of 365). Conversely, if you get one percent worse each day for one year, you'll decline by the end of the year. Small gains made consistently over time can make for a massive improvement.

Most of us love to hear about the rags to riches stories of athletes who came from nothing and made it to the big time. We like to think about these stories as a singular event in time. However, the reality is that these success stories aren't stand-alone events, but rather the sum of all the little moments where the athlete improved bit by bit, over a long period of time. The question then is: what can you start today that will get you a step closer to you where you want to be? What would a one percent improvement each day look like?

THE 10,000 HOUR MYTH

Ok, so you have dedicated to improving at least 1% each day. You might ask: "How long do I keep this up? Do I just put in a certain amount of time and effort and eventually be considered a 'master'?" Not quite. Mastery involves many steps and stages on the way to learning and growth. Rather than focusing on mastery of the skill itself, you need to get good at mastering the pursuit of mastery. This means understanding that it's not just about the amount of time you put in, but how that time is spent. In essence, you must unlearn what you have learned about mastery.

You might be familiar with the 10,000-hour rule, popularized by Malcolm Gladwell in his bestseller *Outliers: The Story of Success* and based on research done by Anders Ericsson[43]. Although it sounds catchy and is easy to remember, this idea was misinterpreted. In fact, Anders Ericsson never explicitly stated that it takes 10,000 hours to master anything. What he and his team of researchers showed was that the number of hours is arbitrary, and what really matters is "deliberate practice." This is a type of practice where we are highly focused, integrating feedback from experts, and working on the correct technique, rather than doing something wrong for an extended period.

The biggest flaw of the 10,000-hour rule is that it focuses on the amount of time spent practicing and not the quality of that practice: not all practice is equally helpful. That is not to say the more hours you put into something won't do you any good, but what matters is that you make the most of the time it takes to pursue mastery. When we get caught up on objective measures like the amount of time spent practicing, we miss out on being fully present in the actual act of practicing.

For example, a novice golfer might think that if they just spent more time practicing their shot, they automatically will become proficient at golf. There is so much more to learning a skill than just the pure mechanics of going through the motions. Practicing an incorrect golf swing for 10,000 hours will just create a slightly better incorrect golf swing.

THE STAGES OF MASTERY

The training I present in this book is not about *adding*, but rather *letting* go of what holds you back, mostly the self-critical and judgemental self that is in the way of doing.

Bruce Lee states this idea as focusing on "simplicity of expression, rather than complexity of form[44]." This is because you already have everything you need inside of you, whether that is to learn new things or to accomplish great things. All it takes is to develop the right trust in this ability.

The first step in this process is to understand the process itself. Mastery is a constant flow of learning and unlearning. We can understand this through a four-stage model that relates to the psychological states involved in mastery. These stages are: unconscious incompetence, conscious incompetence, conscious competence, and unconscious competence[45]. This is illustrated by the pyramid below.

Following this model can help us navigate the complex learning process that takes place on the path to mastery. We are often misguided in thinking that talent is something we are naturally gifted with. Although this may be the case for some individuals, most of us go through stages of trial and error to become proficient. This four-stage model represents what one might experience psychologically going through a learning curve. Let's go over each stage in more detail.

1. **Unconscious Incompetence**

In the first stage of learning, you do not understand or know how to do the task and do not necessarily recognize you do not know how to do it well. You may even deny the usefulness of the particular skill or activity. In this stage, you must recognize and accept your own incompetence and the value of the new skill before moving on and progressing.

The length of time you spend in this stage depends on the strength of the stimulus to learn. As flow doesn't necessarily require high challenge and high skill (although it creates a more intense experience) one can experience flow whilst being low on both. This may be enough to encourage you to pursue the activity again. For example, when you learn to juggle, failure is a prolonged inevitability. But after some practice, you may experience a moment where things briefly click into place; a momentary "aha" moment where a new door of possibility opens. It is at this moment that you take your first steps into a larger world of possibility.

2. Conscious Incompetence

To put it more frankly, at this stage you understand how much you suck. Though you may not understand or know how to do the particular skill with grace or ease, you recognize the deficit as well as the value of this skill and begin addressing the deficit. After some brief encounters with mild competence, you pave the way for more adequate training. Making mistakes is integral to the learning process, as the more you fail the more you learn. For this reason, it is important not to get discouraged by failure at this stage. In other words, while juggling you will drop the balls a lot, but this is normal and isn't a sign that you are bad at juggling.

3. Conscious Competence

With sufficient practice, patience, and time, you may begin to understand how to do the skill. While juggling, you finally hit the point where you can juggle the balls for a period of time, however, demonstrating the skill or knowledge requires concentration and effort. You might break down the skills into steps, such as counting each catch and release of the ball and there is heavy conscious involvement in executing the new skill. You may start to receive feedback from others regarding your newly learned skill which may promote further motivation to continue.

4. Unconscious Competence

The final stage of skill acquisition is the stage of doing without thinking, or in other words, having a mind without mind. You have so much practice with a skill that it has become "second nature" and you can perform it easily and with minimal conscious (thinking) effort. Our thinking self gets out of the way, and the doing takes the stage.

As a result, the skill can even be performed while executing another task since attentional resources can be allocated elsewhere. Keeping with the juggling example, you might even get to a stage where you juggle while riding a unicycle. Moreover, you are able to teach the skill to others, and depending on your skill of communicating this process to others; you may even become a proficient coach or teacher. Flow states may be quite frequent at this stage, but athletes might also experience plateaus. Therefore, it is crucial that you find ways to increase your level of challenge periodically in order to continue to grow and maintain your level of enjoyment. At this level, you can now be considered in the territory of mastery.

MASTERING THE PURSUIT

The goal of pursuing any craft is to reach a stage of unconscious competence, which is essentially having a mind without mind. It is a place where we don't need to necessarily think about doing a skill, but can perform the skill unconsciously, without thinking. In this stage, no amount of overthinking will help you perform better. The body already knows what to do, so all that is left is to get out of one's own way.

In fact, having too much of an internal focus can contribute to choking, a phenomenon any individual involved in high performance is all too familiar with. This emphasis on the self is known as *explicit monitoring* where you focus too much attention on the internal mechanics of a given movement. This results in something sport psychologists call *paralysis by analysis*[46].

An example of this is a baseball pitcher worrying too much about their form, so much so that their arm responds by physically not being able to release the ball at the appropriate time. Do a google search for "the yips" and you will find countless examples of athletes physically not being able to perform a task they have done for years because they've fallen victim to excessive anxiety and an over-emphasis on internal mechanics.

Focusing on yourself is important during the early stages of skill acquisition, but is of little use to the experienced performer. After a certain stage, the experienced individual does not necessarily need to learn anything new but rather needs to unlearn old habits that hinder the natural state of doing the skill. They simply get better at getting out of their own way.

Another contributor to choking is *distraction*. In this case, you might get simply distracted by too many stimuli which are unnecessary for performance. You might start to get self-conscious about how you look, and as such, focus on task-irrelevant cues such as who is in the crowd watching. In fact, researchers found that the presence of audiences impairs performance on complex tasks[47]. Even the most seasoned performer will get caught in this trap of the mind and fall into old thinking patterns. This is normal but can be remedied by the practices outlined in the following chapters.

THE DANGERS OF DUNNING-KRUGER

Something that is more difficult to recognize and can be limiting progression towards mastering a certain skill is the notion that one is already "mentally tough." This type of individual doesn't believe they need to improve on anything. This is a typical trap of the unconscious incompetence stage where individuals tend to be quite confident in their ability. This is so common that researchers David Dunning and Justin Kruger found this phenomenon across domains.

This is now considered a cognitive bias known as the Dunning-Kruger Effect[48]. This is the tendency for novices to underestimate the amount of time and skill required to master something. This is because peoples' incompetence robs them of the metacognitive ability to realize their inadequacy. Their idea of what they believe is required to become skillful at a task is limited by how little they know about that task. We tend to underestimate what there is left to learn and ironically feel more confident than some experts.

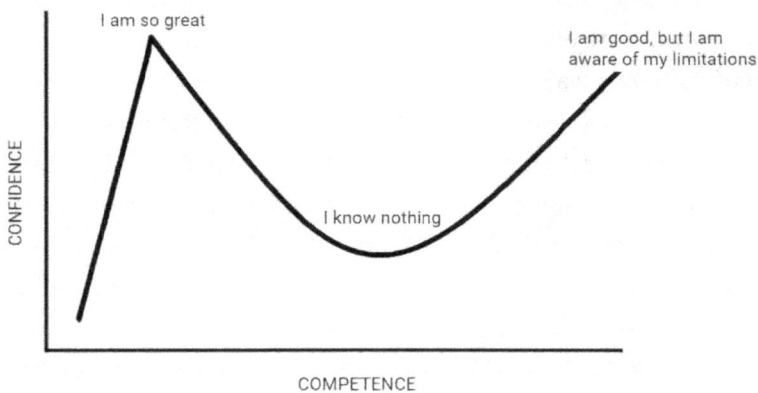

As we progress in skill and in the stages of competence, confidence tends to go down as you start to realize how much more there is to learn. As Aristotle said, "the more you know, the more you know you don't know." This causes a drop in self-efficacy (the belief in oneself). Therefore, as you progress through any skill, be it physical or mental, you might find your confidence going down, and find yourself discouraged. You might even experience something known as "imposter syndrome", the feeling that a lot of experts have that they are frauds, and it's just a matter of time before someone finds them out.

But this feeling is actually a good sign; it means you are finally beginning to understand the complexity that is the mastery process, and this metacognitive shift in perspective allows for a humbler approach.

With time and practice, the idea of how much you don't know will no longer be a hindrance and will free your mind to focus on the things that are within your control. Keep this in mind as you go through this next section. Bringing your limitations to the surface is not a sign of weakness or in any way a failure, but rather the necessary progress one must make in order to call themselves a master—be it of craft, or of self.

We get better at things not by never finding them difficult, but by being aware of, accepting, and identifying the problem. It is only when we incorporate what Zen calls a *beginner's mind,* that we can fully start our journey on the path to mastery. In the beginner's mind, no piece of information is left untouched. This creates a sense of novelty and complexity, which as we know, are massive flow triggers. To quote zen master Shunryo Suzuki:

> *"In the beginner's mind there are many possibilities, but in the expert's, there are few."*[49]

Incorporate this perspective into your mental training and you will never stop learning.

TRAINING YOUR MIND

Peak performance in any field, be it sport, business, academia, music, or any other domain requires the application of knowledge, skills, and ability and, involves a unique set of physical, technical, and strategic skills that one must consistently train and improve. However, one element that most would agree on is the importance of psychological skills, without which true mastery is not possible. Unfortunately, most of us learn this lesson a bit too late, such as when an athlete recognizes how much more they could have done if they had just trained their mind better, or burning themselves out because they didn't learn how to mentally and physically recover.

I understand the struggles of both from first-hand experience.

Training your mind is a necessary requirement if you wish to live out your fullest potential. As Sam Harris, neuroscientist, philosopher, and author of *Waking Up: A Guide to Spirituality Without Religion* puts it:

> *"Some people are content in the midst of deprivation and danger, while others are miserable despite having all the luck in the world. This is not to say that external circumstances do not matter. But it is your mind, rather than circumstances themselves, that determines the quality of your life. Your mind is the basis of everything you experience and of every contribution you make to the lives of others. Given this fact, it makes sense to train it."*[50]

The goal of the next few chapters is to provide you with a framework in which to better understand the psychological conditions for peak performance and flow. There is no manual for guaranteed success, but if we have some tools to work with, we can build something special.

Mental Performance Training follows four main flow conditions that can aid in thinking, feeling, and performing at our very best. If you recall from part one, these four conditions to flow are: the balance between challenge and skill, immediate feedback, setting clear objectives, and complete concentration. The Mental Performance Training (MPT) model is a way to blend all these psychological triggers to flow into a tangible and trainable framework.

The MPT model is divided into 3 parts:

(1) **Self-awareness** which groups together creating a better sense of awareness of the challenge-skill balance, developing a personal philosophy, as well as developing feedback systems in your internal and external environments.

(2) **Clear objectives** covers goal setting and how having a clear purpose and vision gets you closer to living a life that is authentically yours.

(3) **Mindfulness training** deals with ways to develop a deeply focused embodiment in what one is doing.

When you consistently nurture all three parts, you will find yourself more prone to the experience of flow, which, as we know creates enhanced performance, satisfaction, and happiness. This, like any good mental training program, is influenced by the latest research in sport & performance psychology to enhance well-being and performance. The primary goal is to help performers increase their capacity to navigate the stressors, setbacks, and demands of performance. This ultimately increases one's susceptibility to flow state and experiencing a mind without mind.

This mental training program is a blend of my own philosophical, psychological, and scientific insights, that I have learned through my studies and my own practice with flow states.

As I've discussed in this book, patterns of data and anecdotal evidence suggest that certain environmental and psychological traits and conditions can help increase the susceptibility of achieving better performance. The intention of this mental training model, then, is to break down these traits into trainable components. But rather than a scripted and linear process that one can follow in a step-by-step way, this model is designed as a cycle that changes and varies with each new challenge.

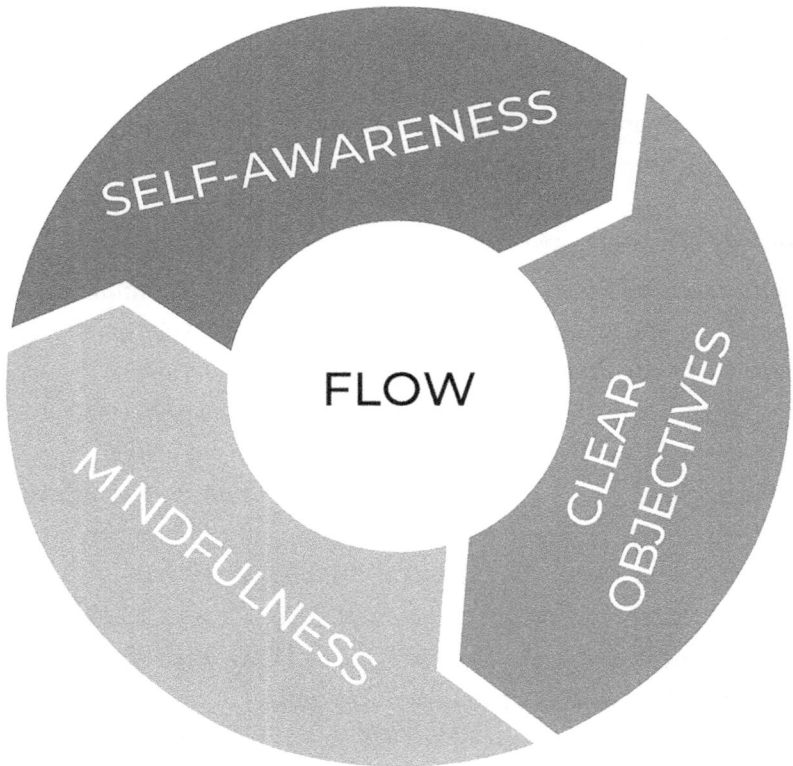

To aid in your training, each section in this book will include an applied exercise or worksheet for you to follow along with and complete (which can be downloaded at www.flowperformancepsych.com/workbook-download), but the real work will be done outside of the pages of this book. Of course, individual needs may vary, and you may have specific concerns about your performance such as performance anxiety, lack of confidence, life transitions, etc. In these cases, a book can only be an added resource, and I recommend that you work with a trained professional who will help you take a deeper dive into your own personal journey. Remember that, just as with any physical training, mental training requires commitment and work, and the only person that can take you to the next level is you. But if you apply time and effort, you too can master the mental game.

RECAP

- You can only control three things about your performance: Your thoughts, your attitude, and your actions. The more you control the controllables, the more space you have for optimal performance. Don't underestimate the power of doing the little things. Even a 1% improvement each day compounds over time.

- The old model of putting in more hours (10,000-hour rule) is not completely accurate. What matters is deliberate, focused, quality practice done over a long period of time. This is the path to mastery, which involves four stages of competence:

1. Unconscious incompetence
2. Conscious competence
3. Conscious competence
4. Unconscious competence

- "Imposter syndrome" is quite normal on the path to mastery. It means you are learning and growing!

- Follow along with the workbook provided: **www.flowperforman-cepsych.com/workbook-download.** The password to access the file is **NoMind2021**.

4

SELF-AWARENESS

When you think of the question, "who am I?", what comes to mind? Is it your chosen craft, your citizenship, or perhaps the name you were given at birth? Is that really all you are?

What I am asking about here isn't the obvious, surface-level stuff, but rather the real, deep-down you. Before we can attain peak performance, we must first fully comprehend who we *really* are. Contrary to what you might think, you are more than just what you do; too many of us struggle with decoupling the *doing* part from the *being*.

Athletes tend to tie their identity with being an athlete. This has benefits, of course, as we tend to spend more time working on the things we identify with and enjoy. However, it does sometimes come with a cost. When your entire concept of self is locked into being an athlete, then every mistake or setback feels like an existential crisis. In these circumstances, our minds tend to paint every mistake or loss as black and white rather than shades of grey. Having a better sense of who you really are outside of your sport will not only enhance your performance but will increase your overall well-being. What is the point of being the best in the world at something if you're not going to like yourself along the way? Let go of the idea that you are what you do. Doing more won't necessarily always get you better results; it tends to lead to burnout and over-identification with a skill that can be taken away from you in an instant.

Instead, we need to learn to separate who we are from what we do. This can be one of the most important skills you can develop in the field of high performance.

You might be wondering; "how does understanding who I really am help me perform at my best?" Well, the relationship you have with yourself is the most important one you will ever cultivate, and without understanding what it means to be your authentic self, you are vulnerable to be defined by someone else's idea of who we should be, such as parents, friends, or society in general. This happens more often than one would expect.

For example, many of the individuals with whom I have had the chance to work could not get to the bottom of why they were playing their particular sport. Some of them did it because their parents forced them to, or they had simply been playing it for so long that it is just how they defined themselves without actually asking whether they enjoyed it anymore. Without getting to the core of who we are and what we want to do, we are likely to just run through the motions, day by day, and then wonder why we're not enjoying our lives very much.

The top performers are the ones who are incredibly clear on what it means to be them, which does not include putting themselves in a box by defining themselves solely as an athlete. They understand that who they are is separate from athletics and other aspects of their lives.

Understanding this fact can be of tremendous power because we are longer shackled down by one-dimensional thinking. In other words, we are not slaves to the consequences of the successes or failures of the sport we started for fun. The more you can just be yourself and let the doing flow, the more you are injected with a strength that no amount of physical training can top. Be more confident, be more present, be more authentic: peak performance will come as a result.

Of course, this is all easier said than done. We all want to be more authentic, but it is quite difficult to decipher what that really means. I don't believe that humans will ever fully be capable of complete awareness of who we are. However, we can take steps towards painting a better picture so that at least we can move in the right direction towards mental mastery. More importantly, we get better at understanding what doesn't work for us which gives us valuable data on our journey towards mental mastery.

CREATING A PERSONAL PHILOSOPHY

Understanding yourself is at the core of reaching mastery in any craft. Without fully grasping who you are both as an individual and as a performer, you will never have a clear enough vision for what goals you want to achieve. Self-awareness is a pre-requisite for setting a clear objective (the next chapter) because it reflects the values that shape and guide the goal-setting process.

For example, if one of your values is about giving back to younger athletes and forming relationships, then your decisions and goals should be made with a piece of this in mind. Without understanding what these values are first, we risk setting goals that are not organically ours, and we tend to lose track of them over time.

Before you go about setting any goals, it is imperative that you are clear on your personal philosophy. Having a concrete philosophy is at the core of any journey of self-actualization. You may be familiar with this term, introduced by psychologist Abraham Maslow in his paper on the hierarchy of needs[51]. Self-actualization refers to the need for personal growth and discovery that is present throughout a person's life. Through the process of self-actualization, a person comes to find an important meaning in their life. Doing all this, of course, is hard work. It is probably the most difficult thing you will do in your life. This is why most people tend to avoid introspection. We do not want to know what is inside our minds, yet alone try and confront it. As Bruce Lee explains:

"Honestly expressing yourself...it is very difficult to do...to express oneself honestly, not lying to oneself...now that, my friend, is very hard to do"

Getting a clear understanding of yourself and your personal philosophy as it pertains to your life and performance will go a long way in laying the foundations for your success. Without being clear on what drives your motivation, you risk falling onto a path that may not be conducive to your performance and well-being.

While you may feel some skepticism and doubt as you go through this section and its various exercises, I welcome you to practice an open, curious, and non-judgemental beginner's mind.

DEFINE YOUR MPP

The first step in our exercise is to define your MPP: Your mission (M), your purpose (P), and your philosophy (P). Your MPP is useful when you are starting the process of creating a framework for self-awareness and mental mastery. Let's take a closer look.

Mission

Start with defining _what_ exactly you want to do with your life. What are some things you want to accomplish in the short or long term? What is important that you complete in your life, performance or non-performance related? What do you want to be known for? When someone writes your eulogy, what would they say?

Purpose

Understanding your _why_ behind the what (aka. the mission) will keep you on track and inspire you to go above and beyond.

Philosophy

This is your guiding principle. Something you base your life on. _How_ exactly will you live out your what and why?

UNDERSTAND YOUR VALUES

Before you can develop your MPP, it is important to understand your core principles and ideals, otherwise known as values. Values are a way of determining what actions are best to do or what way is best to live our lives. Having a clear sense of what your key values are help us course correct whenever we get off track. When we behave in ways that support and align with our core beliefs, we are more likely to stick to the behavior over the long term. For example, people who have organized their values are better positioned to exhibit more self-control when there are two conflicting goals, such as making a decision between immediate pleasure (skip practice to watch movies) and long-term plans (getting a University scholarship).

To begin the MPP process, let's start by identifying some words or phrases that represent who you are that will guide your process of creating a set of values. These values will be the pillars that hold up your mission, purpose, and ultimate philosophy. Your goal is to get to five core values (pillars) that represent who you are. But don't worry if you can't boil down your life into just five key values; trust me, it's hard work. The intent is to start chipping away at identifying what's important to you, piece by piece until you have a more defined list of the most important values by which you want to live. Many of our values will change over time, but the ones that stick around are worth noting.

Let's start by just writing down 10-20 words or phrases that really cut to the core of what it means to be you. Get out a piece of paper and answer the following prompts or use the worksheet available for download. No need to overthink them, just write down what feels authentic.

1. What are 10-20 words, phrases or themes, that cut to the core of what it means to be you? *(eg. health, creativity, enjoyment, power, love, flow, stillness, authenticity, family).*
2. Why did you pick these values, and why are they important to you?
3. If you had to trim your list from 5 down to 1 value, what would it be? *One technique is to fill in these blanks with the first word or phrase that pops into your head: It all comes down to_____ or I am_____.*
4. Based on the values you have chosen; can you craft a **MISSION** statement? *(think **what** you want to do or accomplish with your chosen values. Eg. "to become a master of my craft through creativity, passion, and cultivating my relationships")*
5. **Why** do you want to do it? What is your **PURPOSE**? *(I want to do this because...)*
6. **How** will you live out your mission and purpose? This will be your personal **PHILOSOPHY** *(Keep it short and simple. For example, mine is: Live Slow. Find Flow).*

What did you notice when doing this exercise? Was it easy or challenging? Perhaps you have decided to come back to it another time, and that is totally fine. But at least some gears were starting to turn, and this is the intention behind the exercise. Slowly but surely what was blurry will become clear and you will increase your level of self-awareness.

Using visual metaphors can be very useful in portraying your vision. If you're a visual thinker like me, you may find it more fruitful to use the aid on the next page to create your personal philosophy.

Start with writing your core values from the exercise above in the five pillars. Then, write your philosophy (how you are going to go about living your mission and values) on the base. The clearer and more succinct it is, the easier it will be to use it on a daily basis. For example, it could be: "Always strive for excellence", or "Be authentically yourself."

The mission or purpose goes on top. This is the ultimate objective for your life or performance. Think of it in whatever terms you wish, but if we are clear on what we ultimately want our life to be like then how we achieve our goals comes much more organically.

For example, the company Headspace (Creators of the meditation app of the same name) is very clear on theirs: *to improve the health and happiness of the world.* You don't have to go that global just yet. Simplify your mission statement to suit your needs. If you are really looking for clarity, see if you can focus your 5 pillars into just 3.

Exercise: <u>Develop your personal values and philosophy</u>

Using the worksheet provided, come up with your MPP, and list up to 5 core values that feel authentic to you. Here is an example:

Core Values: Mastery, creativity, relationships, autonomy, playfulness

Mission/Purpose: To help bring out the best in others

Philosophy: I will seek happiness and success will follow

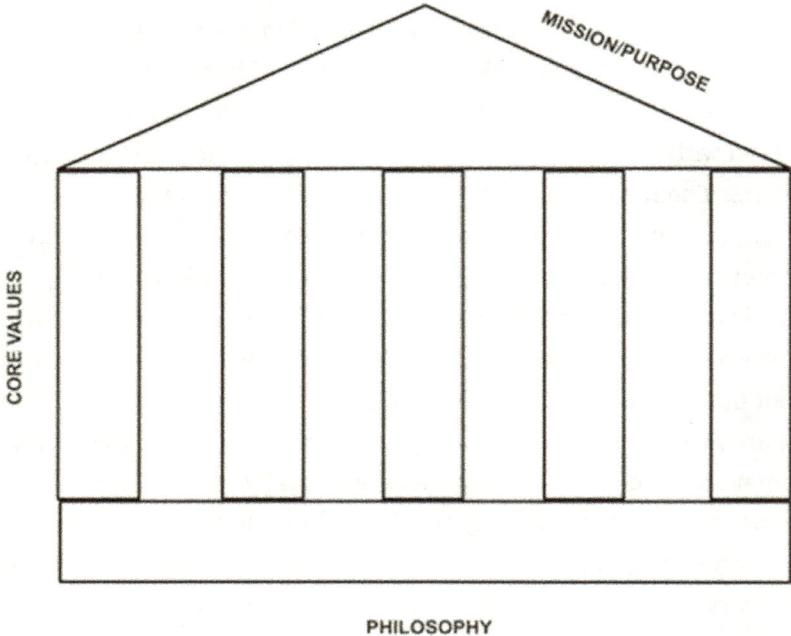

IDENTIFYING YOUR BARRIERS

Once we are clearer on our personal philosophy and values, it is important to reflect on any barriers holding us back from living a life aligned with them. The following exercise is designed to bring to the surface any mental, physical, or technical barriers that currently keep you from performing your best. When we identify and accept the barriers holding us back, we can implement the necessary training to overcome them, be it mental or physical.

As with the previous exercise, you may use a piece of paper, or use the corresponding worksheet in the link provided. To begin, list any specific barriers that you know are currently impacting your life and/or performance. These could be things like performance anxiety, lack of confidence, financial issues, worry, dissatisfaction with coaches, etc. The purpose is to bring them to the surface and shed some light on them so you may become more aware and tackle the ones you can control. For example, you might experience some of the following:

- Currently experiencing a run of bad form and not being able to "find your game"
- Juggling school or work while being a full-time athlete
- Not being able to afford the various expenses associated with your sport, such as travel, accommodation, or food
- Being cut from a team and having an identity crisis

When we put pen to paper and physically write out things that are bothering us, we step away from the issues and can see them right in front of us. They become more objective and less frightening. This way, we develop a greater sense of self-awareness.

Exercise: List your performance barriers

What is currently holding you back from performing at your best? Is it physical, mental, social? List any barriers to your performance that come to mind in point form using the worksheet provided, or on a piece of paper.

* * *

EXPLORING YOUR BARRIERS

Next, you need to get familiar with what particular performance domain is being affected the most by the barriers that you have listed. Some performance domains we might be interested in exploring are:

- Practise/Training
- Competition
- Relationships with coaches
- Relationships with teammates
- Friends/Family

Using the worksheet provided, you will find columns next to each performance domain. These columns are "level of perceived challenge" and "level of perceived skill." Here, you will rate yourself in each category from 1-10 (1 being low perceived challenge and skill, and 10 being high challenge and skill). For example, you may feel that in the competition domain you feel an 8 challenge when actively competing, while your perceived level of skill is at a 6. This indicates that you may be more anxious in this particular domain.

For the domain of relationships, think about the quality of how your relationship is with this particular person or group (friends and family), and reflect on your ability to effectively manage these relationships positively. For instance, you may have a difficult coach who increases your level of perceived challenge in training, but perhaps you are confident in your skill of handling his or her coaching style. Here is an example of how your table might look like:

Rate each performance domain from 1-10 (1 = low / 10 = high) in each column

PERFORMANCE DOMAIN	LEVEL OF PERCEIVED CHALLENGE	LEVEL OF PERCEIVED SKILL
Practise/Training	7	7
Competition	9	7
Relationships with coaches	8	6
Relationships with teammates	5	6
Friends/Family	2	5
Other: SCHOOL	8	6

Exercise: Figure out your challenge-skill ratio

Rate each performance domain from 1-10 in terms of your perceived level of challenge and skill. High challenge can be seen as both positive and negative, depending on your ability to manage the perceived demands. Some domains pertain to your performance, such as competition, while other domains, such as relationships with coaches, are about your ability to manage complex interactions.

* * *

Once you have completed this, you will start to notice some patterns. Maybe you perform better in training than you do in competition, or that your relationship with your coach could use some work. Keep in mind the performance barriers you listed earlier. Do they have an impact on any of these areas? For example, if your performance barrier of feeling pressure from your coach was not there, would the challenge go down? The goal here is to get clear on what exactly is impacting your performance in a negative way.

CHALLENGE-SKILL BALANCE

The next step is to be honest with yourself: are you lacking challenge, or skill in each of these domains? Do you feel like you have too much on your plate right now, or too little? Energized, or burned out? It might be useful for you to visualize this. Using the challenge-skill graph provided in the worksheets, markdown where you feel you are based on your answers in the previous exercise. You may separate different performance domains, or rate yourself in general. If it is helpful to you, view each axis as a score from 1-10 and follow the line.

Exercise: Visualize the challenge-skill ratio

Using the challenge-skill graph, mark the location where your challenge and skill intersect. Do you find yourself more in the "anxiety" zone, "boredom" zone, or in the "flow channel"? For example, if you feel your perceived level of skill is at a 4, and the challenge you feel is at a 9 then mark it in the spot where the two overlap.

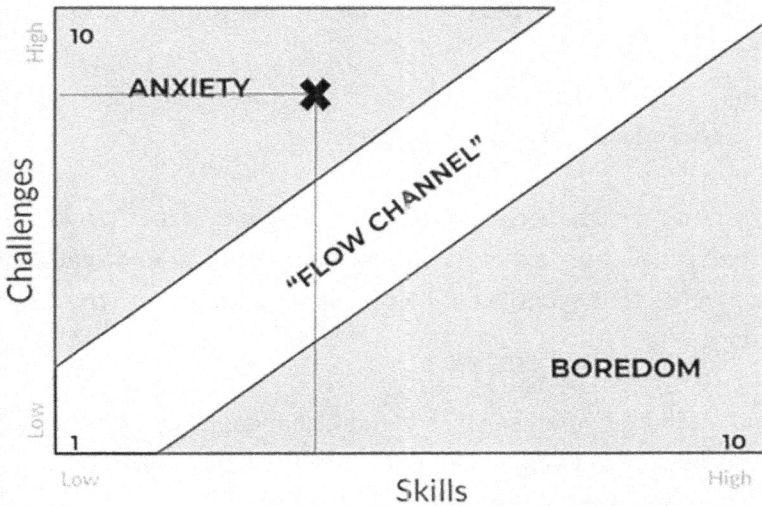

* * *

Having a balance between challenge and skill is a crucial ingredient to optimal motivation and attention. As I discussed earlier, the general rule of thumb is to have challenge around 4% higher than your skill level, as it is just outside of our comfort zone where we can learn and grow without being too overwhelmed.

Perhaps you are feeling a bit bored with the way your performance is going. You are not challenged enough in training to engage you. Or maybe you are feeling way too anxious. Either way, by completing this exercise, you have taken your first step to greater self-awareness. Just admitting the fact that you are overwhelmed is progress in itself.

Most individuals struggle with this first crucial step of identifying the barriers to their performance and it prevents them from moving forward. Whatever you are currently experiencing is completely normal, and more importantly, does not define who you are or your ability to perform.

Exercise: <u>Reflect on the following questions:</u>

If you don't feel challenged enough (bored), why is that? If you feel too much challenge (anxiety) which performance barrier do you think is in play? Refer to your list of performance barriers from the earlier exercise.

If you feel bored, how can you add more challenge to your activity so you can be around 4% challenged? If you feel too anxious, how can you reduce some of the challenge?

* * *

It might be difficult to visualize what an increase of 4% actually looks like. For me, I know I am getting close to 4% when I start to feel some anxiety, but I am able to stay in control of my thoughts and actions. If I don't feel any nervousness it means the activity isn't demanding enough. For example, I can feel a difference in my ability whenever I run on technical trails in dry or wet conditions. The wet and slippery trails create an increased challenge, but not too much that I feel like I don't have enough skill to keep up.

If you find yourself too challenged in a particular performance domain, research suggests that focusing on the "how" can be effective. When a task is too challenging, it is better to identify an action or behaviour on a lower level of difficulty, which means breaking down the actions into smaller, concrete "how-to" steps. In the case of my trail running, for example, I need to physically slow down and plan my footsteps carefully to avoid a mudslide or any roots.

In contrast, when challenge is too low, focusing on the "why" can motivate someone to do better. In other words, writing out how to pursue your goal leads to better performance when you have lower domain-specific skills, and writing about why to pursue a goal leads to better performance when your domain-specific skills are higher[52]. Continuing with the trail running example, I can create more motivation to run on a treadmill when I reframe it as training for the more difficult and complex trail runs. This way the treadmill run has a specific purpose and clear "why."

CREATING A FEEDBACK SYSTEM

In order to experience growth, we must make sure it is the activity we are making more challenging, and not the interface, tool, or instrument. In the case of our performance, the interface can be ourselves, and the tools are our perception and self-talk. This is where it is important to make sure our systems of feedback are tailored toward progression and not regression. To achieve this, we must have a system of course correction to move towards a more manageable and ultimately fulfilling journey.

As we know, feedback is a crucial trigger for flow. Without feedback, you can't measure and track progress. To increase the likelihood of flow, feedback must be immediate and unambiguous. If feedback is not immediate, we start to look for things we've done in the past, or compare ourselves to others, both of which pull us out of the present moment. Therefore, we need to create a system where the feedback we receive is reinforcing positive behaviour and improvement.

Of course, feedback can be tough to come by in many cases. We cannot control how often our coach gives us direction (or the correct direction for that matter) and so we are sometimes unable to reduce the gap between our inputs (eg. Executing a training drill) and the output (eg. Results of a given action or behaviour). The feedback we get from others is important as it holds a lot of weight, but unfortunately, it is outside of our control since it is external.

For example, if you are a tennis player, your coach may provide you with specific feedback on your shot. It is not always immediate, but it provides you with good information to correct and adjust your technique. Adding video to the mix would create a bit more immediacy to the feedback since you are watching yourself in real-time. A good coach will make use of both methods in order to reduce the input-output gap. Another example of *immediate* external feedback is whether the ball goes where it's supposed to go or not. This provides you with a lot more objectively accurate information on how you're doing. We can summarize external feedback this way:

External feedback

- *High impact*
- *Varying time gap between input & output*
- *Low degree of control*
- *Eg. coach instruction, win/lose, game tape*

However, we must also find ways to keep ourselves in check in the absence of external feedback. For example, perhaps your coach only provides you with feedback at the end of practice. Because we can't control our coach's feedback style, we need to create a system of *internal* feedback. Internal feedback has a lower impact initially, but it has a high degree of control and tends to be immediate.

Internal feedback

- *Low to moderate impact (initially)*
- *Immediate*
- *High degree of control*
- *Eg. the way you speak to yourself*

The feedback you give yourself (i.e. the things you tell yourself) is an example of internal feedback. The things you tell yourself can have a positive influence on the outcome over time. If you form a habit of positive, specific, and immediate direction after each play it will soon start to have a greater impact. Therefore, after each attempted shot, regardless of whether it went in or out, your feedback should be guiding your attention to the present and be guiding your performance, not degrading it. This is important because although the ball placement gives us useful external cues, where the ball goes once it leaves your racket is not 100% inside your control. Internal feedback is absolutely inside your control.

INTERNAL FEEDBACK
(INNER DIALOGUE)

Become aware of negative dialogue.
Change the narrative.
Eg. "You got this"; "Keep pushing"

Get caught up in the stream of thought
(too many mind). Judge yourself for doing so.
Eg. "I am horrible.."; "Why am I always so negative"

An athlete can say the same statement in two different ways. For example, saying *"you didn't follow through on your backhand!"* can be applied in a harsh degrading tone, or can be said as more of an observation. The latter style provides you with information and helps improve rather than lower self-esteem.

Exercise: List your internal feedback sources

What are your current internal methods of feedback? Is the feedback you give yourself helping or hindering your performance? Write down the typical self-talk statements you say to yourself. Bringing them to the surface will increase your self-awareness. For example: "Judging each failed shot with a harsh, degrading negative self-talk impacts my ability to concentrate and stay positive."

Once you have made your list reflect on what is or isn't working.

* * *

Although it is more difficult, we can also apply the same technique to the external feedback we receive. We cannot control what is given to us, but we are able to choose our response to the given feedback. Having a more open, and receptive mindset will help you improve, as you will be less defensive when your coach or others give you negative feedback. This is also known as a *growth mindset*, popularized by researcher Dr. Carol Dweck. Dr. Dweck found that an openness to constructive feedback has been shown to be a very strong predictor of success in life. People with a *fixed mindset*, on the other hand, have the belief that attributes are fixed rather than learned, and are often not open to receiving feedback from others because they don't believe they can change their approach or performance[53]. The type of response we have to feedback is always within our control, so we must make sure we apply a growth mindset to learn and grow.

NOT IN OUR CONTROL

NOT IN OUR CONTROL   *IN* OUR CONTROL

Approach constructive criticism with
an open mind. Apply the lessons.
(GROWTH MINDSET)

RECEIVED FEEDBACK
(EXTERNAL)

Become defensive and stucky in your ways. Do not
utilize feedback for growth. After all you know best!
(FIXED MINDSET)

INCORPORATING FEEDBACK

Ultimately, we want to bridge the gap between internal and external feedback systems. Creating a positive and meaningful dialogue within yourself is important to well-being and performance, and the great thing about this is that it is always within your control, and at your disposal. Combined with having more external feedback, it can be a powerful tool to move you towards greater self-awareness. Find ways to receive as much information about your performance as possible by asking coaches, teammates, friends, or family to evaluate you. Be sure to be open to their feedback, as even if it might seem negative it could be a doorway to something you've never noticed before.

Feedback is a potent flow trigger. This is why performers in domains that have a shorter input-output gap, like comedy or music, tend to experience a lot of flow. There is nothing clearer and more definitive than others' laughter. If the joke is bad, you will know right away. While seeing the crowd dancing is another form of feedback that tells the band whether their music has been positively received or not. Clear markers that guide your performance open some space in which to operate and course-correct in real-time.

Some sports and activities are naturally wired for immediate feedback. A golfer, curler, or archer gets immediate feedback that their shot skewed way too far left, for example. But in most cases, feedback can be hard to come by. We can't control what our coach tells us, or perhaps we don't even have someone to give us the feedback we need. Take a moment to reflect on what sources of external feedback are available to you.

Exercise: List your external feedback sources

What are your current external methods of feedback? How effective are they? How much control do you have over each?

Once you have made your list, reflect on how you can improve your external resources, such as seeking better quality feedback from a more trusted source, or simply increasing the amount of sources you receive feedback from.

* * *

It is difficult to control anything external to us. There are only three things we have control over: our thoughts, attitude, and actions. How we *think* affects how we *feel*, and ultimately how we *perform*. Thoughts are an internal method of feedback that we all have the potential to use, but you may not be aware of what you say to yourself. Internal feedback might initially have low impact, but with time, it can be used as a powerful tool to build confidence and drive attention to the here and now. Having the right thoughts builds positive habits that guide your attention to what needs to be done, rather than wasting cognitive energy on unnecessary things (such as being self-critical).

The things we tell ourselves impact our attention. For example, if I tell you *don't think of a pink elephant,* what do you think happens? You probably thought of a pink elephant. The same thing applies to performance, such as telling yourself "don't miss", "don't fall", or "don't screw up." If you tell your mind not to do something, you are more likely to focus on the failure. If we don't give the mind something concrete and task-oriented to focus on, it usually ends up focusing on something negative by default. This is because we are wired biologically to scan the environment for threats. It served us well when running away from predators as our ancestors did, but nowadays most of our threats are imagined. This leaves our minds scattered and unfocused.

The way we cope with negative internal feedback is to give the mind something more concrete and positive to focus on instead. Whenever we feel distracted by a negative thought, we can use what is called a *cue word;* a short, simple phrase that triggers an immediacy of attention to the task at hand. An example of this could be "clear the mechanism", "focus", "drive", or my personal favourite "stay frosty", which helps me stay calm and cool under pressure. Giving your mind a cue can help drive attention to the now and let go of the distracting negative thinking.

Exercise: Create a cue word

Pick a cue word or phrase that can help you focus in the moment. What has worked in the past? Think of something you can use during an actual performance situation, such as "let go" or "W.I.N" (What's Important Now). Write it down someplace where you will see it during your performance or your pre-performance routine, such as on your water bottle or in your locker.

* * *

SORT OUT YOUR OBSTACLES

As you may be well aware by now, there are many variables outside of your control in life and performance. Are you focusing on the right ones? How many of the barriers you listed in the first exercise are within your control? How important are they? For example, your coach's opinion might be important to you, but you can't control that. Your effort in training however is very much in your control and equally as important. Sorting where to expend your energy is crucial if you are to make progress without burning yourself out. If you waste energy trying to change things that are simply not within your control, then you risk dissatisfaction with performance and thus lowered performance.

To end this section on self-awareness, solidify your understanding of this concept by mapping out the areas in your sport that are controllable, and which things you can let go of. What is important now, and what is within your control? Use the worksheet provided or draw the table below on a piece of paper. While you do this exercise, you might find that you are unnecessarily emphasizing an unimportant area, such as other people's opinions. What others think of you is out of your control, yet we tend to focus so much of our attention on this. Letting go of this weight can help you spend energy on the important things.

Exercise: Sort out your obstacles

What aspects of your performance are important to you, and within your control? Which ones are not important and within your control? In each box, place a few things that come to mind (eg. Important + out of your control = coach's feedback \ Not important + out of your control = what others say.)

	IMPORTANT	NOT IMPORTANT
WITHIN OUR CONTROL		
OUT OF OUR CONTROL		

* * *

Self-awareness is a foundational skill that requires patience, deep introspection, and an openness to feedback. Developing a personal philosophy, utilizing internal and external feedback, and sorting out your various barriers and obstacles is the first stop on the road to mastery. Make sure you are actively cultivating self-awareness on a regular basis. Take up journaling, or spend some time on a weekly or monthly basis to check in on yourself and see how far you've progressed. Use the challenge-skill graph exercise you completed in the middle of this chapter to visualize how much anxiety or boredom you are currently experiencing.

Self-awareness is an on-going process that requires constant maintenance. Without understanding who you are and what puts you into flow, you risk just going through the motions. Flow activities are freely chosen and are intimately related to the source of what is ultimately meaningful to you, and as such are a precise indicator of who you really are. Self-awareness will be your greatest strength not only as an athlete but as an individual in pursuit of self-actualization.

RECAP

- Developing self-awareness is one of the most important skills anyone can have. The clearer you are on what it means to be you, the easier it is to set goals towards your vision.

- Having a go-to personal philosophy and defined values makes your plan more tangible.

- Understanding your ratio of challenge to skill will help you understand what steps to take to meet your performance goals. If you feel too challenged, then it is time to reduce this perceived challenge through your own self-talk, or changing your physical environment.

- Feedback is one of the crucial ingredients to improve performance and experience flow. Be sure to incorporate both internal and external methods of feedback.

- Using a cue word – a phrase/mantra that is unique to you – can help you refocus on the task at hand. Make sure it is visible to reinforce it.

5

CLEAR OBJECTIVES

You most likely are familiar with goals. Perhaps you love them. Or maybe you don't believe in them. But, being an athlete, you most likely have some sort of target or vague idea of what success looks like for you. This dream or vision is out in the near or distant future and you would like to get that thing or be in that place one day. The previous chapter on self-awareness helped you start the process of painting a poignant picture of what that might entail. In this chapter, we will explore how to set tangible actions and behaviours in order to make that dream a reality.

We do this by setting goals and objectives for ourselves. The key though is to not set targets based on objectives that are set for you by something external, but rather that are in line with your values, or as close to them as possible. In other words: we set goals for ourselves.

Goal setting is the process in which we put our values into action. If done correctly it drives our attention to the present moment and creates conditions for flow and mastery to occur. It's about having a specific action plan, rather than just a general sense of what you want to do. In fact, results from a review of the effects of goal setting on performance show that in 90% of the studies, specific and challenging goals led to higher performance than "do your best" goals, or no goals whatsoever[54]. For such a simple act, the potential for increased performance is well worth pursuing.

For example, if you want to improve your points per game average, it's not enough to just say you want to "be better." You need to set concrete, clear objectives for each competition that involve tangible targets such as getting a certain number of passes or shots each game and having ways to consistently track it over time so that you know how much you improved.

As philosopher Seneca once wrote

"If a man knows not what port he sails to, no wind is favourable."

PROCESS VERSUS OUTCOME GOALS

If your goals are focused on the end result, such as a gold medal or personal best, your mind is essentially disconnected from your body. You are off in a future that has not yet come to fruition. However, when you focus on the task at hand, and on clear and tangible objectives, you are more likely to achieve the result you wanted.

There is evidence to back this up. Individuals with more of a task orientation (a mindset of focusing on things that are associated with the task at hand) increase their effort and persistence when faced with a challenge. Outcome (or ego) oriented individuals, on the other hand, tend to perceive a challenge as a personal lack of ability and assess situations more unfavorably, which results in less effort and persistence in the face of obstacles[55].

Goal orientation also significantly relates to feedback-seeking activities. Individuals with a task orientation are more likely to actively seek out feedback, which as we know from the previous chapter is another crucial ingredient for flow. Thus, setting more process or task-focused goals is more likely to bring the outcome that you want since you can focus on the things that actually get you a step closer to the target, and more importantly are within your scope of control. Hence, it is crucial that we set our goals in a process-oriented way, as opposed to setting goals solely attached to the outcome.

To help put the values that you created in the self-awareness chapter to action, we will move onto creating what I like to call macro (medium to long term) and micro (short term, immediate moment) plans that keep your vision and philosophy in mind. Think of the process as a pyramid, with the base of the pyramid being self-awareness. This is the foundation that goals can be built upon. Then, we layer it with our macro and micro plans. Let's go over a goal-setting technique that I like to call the 100-Day Plan that incorporates all of these elements into a framework for planning your performance.

MACRO GOALS 2
What guides my
day/week/month?

1 MICRO GOALS
What guides the next
immediate moment?

3 SELF AWARENESS
What guides my life?

THE 100-DAY PLAN

Our brains don't like big, overwhelming tasks. It takes up too much cognitive energy to plan every detail for the future. Instead, break down your long-term goals into smaller little chunks with a few concrete actionable steps. You do this by setting macro and micro goals.

One effective goal-setting method is called the 100-Day plan. It is a framework for setting these appropriate macro and micro goals. Kevin Roberts, CEO of Saatchi & Saatchi talks about setting 100-day goals in the book *Peak Performance: Business Lessons from the World's Top Sports Organizations*: "Getting started is deceptively simple. First list around 10 things you need to achieve over the next 100 days. Start each plan with an Action Verb and use no more than 3 words each. Make sure each action is measurable and that each one is a stretch. You'll know when something is a real stretch and when you're just creating a list with things you can tick off."[56]

My version of the 100-day plan breaks down the year into three blocks of time in which we set macro goals such as increasing strength. We then break these macro goals further into micro process goals such as going to the gym three times extra a week. Focusing on these specific goals will ultimately get us closer to the overall outcome.

Let's say you have an outcome goal of making a certain team or winning a championship. Most people would leave their goal-setting at that and call it a day. What we need to do instead, is break that goal down into smaller chunks. With this, we break down your entire year into 3 blocks of 100 days.

But wait! *Doesn't a year have 365 days,* you might ask? *Doesn't this leave us with 65 days left over?* Yes, well done. But don't worry—it will be our little secret. Block 3 will have 100 + 65 days.

Each block has a theme or *macro goal* that will be the focus of that particular block and will increase your chances of meeting your desired outcome.

We then break the macro down even further into more process steps or *micro-goals* that are actionable and can be checked off the list. In the example below, the outcome goal for this athlete is to make the University basketball team next year. In order to do so, this athlete came up with 3 main focus areas that will increase their chances of making the team:

1. Increase strength
2. Increase focus
3. Improve shot percentage.

These goals are a lot more within our control compared to making the team, which has many variables affecting the result (such as other competition, the fact that the coach picks the team, etc.). By keeping these as your main focus rather than the end result, you're much more likely to reach your ideal outcome.

The micro process goals are the things you can actually do in order to complete each block. Ultimately, we are flipping the outcome model on its head. We start with the most basic, tangible thing we can do that helps us get a step closer to the outcome, without ever focusing on the outcome. We begin with the outcome in mind but then break it down further into the most actionable steps possible.

| OUTCOME GOAL: Make the University Team | | |

MACRO **100** Approx. 3 months (14 weeks) **INCREASE STRENGTH**	**MACRO** **100** Approx. 3 months (14 weeks) **IMPROVE FOCUS**	**MACRO** **100(+65)** Approx. 5 months (24 weeks) **IMPROVE SHOT PERCENTAGE BY 15%**
MICRO EXAMPLE: Go to gym 3-4 times per week	**MICRO** EXAMPLE: Meditate 10 minutes each day	**MICRO** EXAMPLE: Shoot 100 extra shots after each practise and keep a log

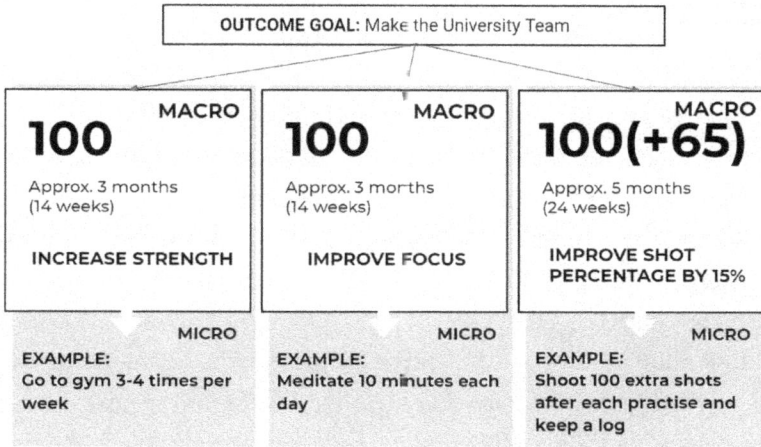

In the example above, going to the gym 3-4 times a week is within your control, which will help you increase strength, and ultimately increasing strength gives you a better shot at making the team. This is just one example of the micro-goals that support the macro.

In the 100-day plan, you will create up to 10 micro (process) goals for each macro goal that will get you closer to the ultimate outcome.

But don't fret if you are not sure whether the micro goals are ambitious enough. The good thing about this method is that the process is designed to be flexible. Pick three dates throughout each block (usually 25, 50, 75 days in) where you come back to the goal, review, and adjust accordingly. For example, say you review your goals 25 days in and find going to the gym 3-4 times per week is too challenging. Adjust it to a more realistic target such as 2-3 times a week. You might also increase the challenge if you find the goal too easy. Using the challenge-skill balance ratio as your guide for self-reflection, find the appropriate goals to set.

MAPPING OUT YOUR NEXT 100 DAYS

To start, get a blank piece of paper and think about what your main objective is for the next 365 days. You don't have to start this at the beginning of the year: you can start at any time.

Once you have your main outcome goal, write it at the top of the page and then create three different blocks of 100 days each (with Block 3 having 165 days).

Think about a subgoal that can go underneath the main outcome. This is your macro goal that will be the main focus for the next 100 days. In the example above, Block 1's macro goal was to increase strength. A good goal to have, but it obviously lacks something tangible and measurable. When you've chosen a macro goal, break it down into smaller steps. These micro goals are how you will go about reaching your macro goal. For instance, going to the gym 3-4 times a week will help increase strength, which in turn will help you make the University team.

Once you have come up with your goals, you can use the 100-Day Plan template provided in the download link (www.flowperforman-cepsych.com/workbook-download) to outline your three Blocks.

You have two options for how to set your goals: create 10 process goals that specifically tie into your outcome or pick 10 things you would like to accomplish in the next 100 days. This all depends on what outcome you have in mind. For example, if you have a specific goal of making a team next year, then perhaps creating 10 process goals will be more useful. If you don't have a clear objective in mind, go back to the drawing board and list a few things you would like to accomplish. Start broad and narrow it down until you have a target to work towards. Don't worry if it isn't perfect just yet, you can always change it. In fact, it's advisable that you change your goals because unexpected events always happen. Your goals shouldn't be a burden but rather used as guideposts for your progress. Make sure to make them flexible and adjust them as needed.

If halfway through your goals, you realize they are too easy or too challenging, then change them! It may take some time for you to get the hang of it, but eventually, you will find a system that works best for you. Be sure to be patient with yourself and don't get discouraged if you don't improve immediately. Remember that small progress is still progress, and it is even worthwhile to focus on a 1% improvement each day.

Exercise: Goal-set using the 100-Day Plan

Using the 100-Day Plan worksheet provided in the workbook, write down an outcome goal for the next 100 days, as well as ten micro (process) goals that get you closer to reaching that outcome. Remember to keep them process-oriented, as well as something that you have full control over. You can use three separate sheets for the three different blocks of the year.

* * *

PERFORMANCE PROFILING

When going through the 100-day plan, you may start to realize that some goals are difficult to measure and track, in particular subjective skills such as focus, confidence, or recovery. To help add a bit more objectivity to some of our goals it can be useful to add a tool used in sport psychology called *performance profiling.*

Performance profiling is used to identify and organize training and to measure development[57]. It can be an effective tool for raising self-awareness of your current ability and enhancing your adherence to different interventions.

Performance profiling creates a visual representation of skill progression in a variety of performance components. The Four Pillars of Performance model (technical, tactical, physical, mental) allows us to pick three attributes or skills in each category and rate ourselves from 1-10. This is visualized in a wheel like this:

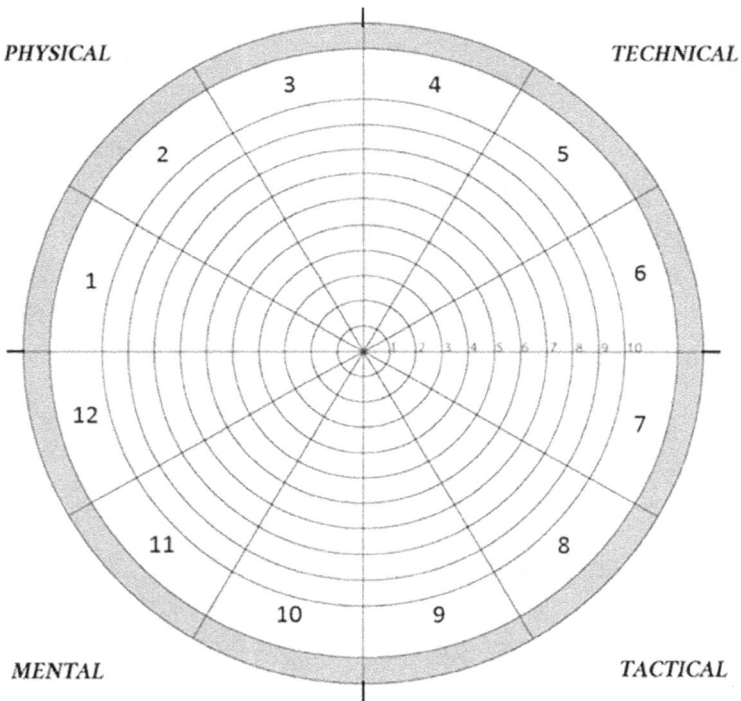

Performance profiling can be used in conjunction with the 100-day plan as an additional tool to help you pick out targets for yourself and to have a system of tracking your progress. For example, if you're a soccer player, you might write down "dribbling" or "passing" as a skill that you would like to improve in the physical pillar. You'd then shade portions of the wheel to show how you would rate yourself from a 1–10 scale (There is a performance profile template in the workbook).

Ratings should be relative to a scale that is realistic to your situation. For example, a fourteen-year-old soccer player should not be comparing themselves to Leonel Messi or Robert Lewandowski. Instead, they should base ratings on their age and level of play. More effective performance profiling takes place when your "ideal" performer competes at a similar level, therefore providing a more realistic target to aim for.

Another important piece to consider with performance profiling is to use it as a way to create more external feedback loops to increase self-awareness. To do this we can ask for feedback from others, such as coaches or teammates to rate us on the various attributes and skills we listed in our performance profile. Sitting down with someone and having a discussion about each attribute can be a useful way to increase your awareness of your skills.

The reason we seek feedback from others is that our perceptions of ourselves tend to be biased and quite inaccurate. We either rate ourselves too high on a given skill (males tend to do this more often) or too low (more common with females).

Receiving constructive criticism on your skills is understandably difficult. We can tend to get defensive, causing communication to break down which can undermine our performance. But learning to handle feedback is necessary for developing true self-awareness and optimal performance. This ability is known as *emotional intelligence (EI)*, defined as the capacity to be aware of, control, and express one's emotions, and to handle interpersonal relationships thoughtfully and empathetically.

Studies on EI have shown that it can lead to greater performance and leadership skills and can even be considered a better predictor of success than general intelligence[58].

An important aspect of emotional intelligence is the ability to have an accurate self-perception of your own abilities and how they are being perceived by others. In a study done at the Institute for Health and Human Potential (IHHP), researchers took a look at 12,256 individuals who rated themselves on certain skills while also being rated by their managers, peers, clients, friends, and family with what is called the EI360 instrument. The EI360 takes a 360-degree look at one's ability to perform in difficult, high-pressure environments.

What they found was quite interesting: Individual's self-ratings were *not* related to performance. Those who rated themselves the *highest* on the listed skills had the *lowest* peer-reviewed scores[59]!

Given this fact, it is critical that we implement feedback with a growth mindset and not get discouraged by a mismatch of self and other ratings. Viewing feedback from others as valuable data can be the first step towards greater development and self-awareness. Using performance profiling and implementing a process-oriented method of goal setting (such as the 100-Day Plan) can help set the stage for these improvements.

Exercise: Create a Performance Profile

Using the Performance Profiling worksheet provided in the workbook, list 12 attributes that you would like to improve (three from each pillar of performance). Rate yourself on each of them from 1-10. Then, pick three people that you would like to get feedback from and ask them to rate you on the skills or attributes you selected.

Compare your self-scores to the scores others gave you and average them out to get an overall performance profile score (add up your score with all the others and divide by the number of scores. Eg. 8 + 7+ 7+ 6 = 28. 28/4= 7 average score).

* * *

THE RULE OF THREE

When done correctly, goals drive our attention to the present. But it is sometimes hard to remember your big goals in the middle of a stressful competition. Therefore, being clear on your micro or process goals can be particularly useful. Having a clear definition of what to do next drives attention to the task at hand, and ultimately the here and now. This is why clear objectives are such an important flow trigger: they give the mind something to focus on. Without any clear target, we risk veering off track.

Once we have established our process goals for the outcome, we can dig a little deeper and get clear on the next immediate step that we need to make in order to keep the momentum going. For example, in the example previously discussed, the athlete's macro goal was to increase strength, where the corresponding micro-goals were to go to the gym three to four times per week specifically working on strength building.

But we can go a little further with this and set micro goals for when we are physically in the gym. This could mean targeting specific muscle groups, a length of time, or spending time mentally preparing. This way the athlete has set an intention for the time spent in the gym, which allows for greater focus. Essentially it is a process within a process, getting down to the little details that are within your control in that given moment.

A useful framework to implement this is something I call the *Rule of Three*. This rule is a quick reference that you can use in real-time to remind you of the process that leads to a larger outcome.

Say you are in the locker room before a big competition and are starting to feel the jitters. All your hard work has gotten you to this point, but you are finding your mind drifting a bit, doubting your ability. Clearly, the outcome is to win the game, or at least to have a great performance. However, focusing on the outcome just creates more tension and anxiety because with this mindset, success is determined by whether or not you win. Instead, you can think of just three things that are process-oriented that will help you achieve your goal. This can lower anxiety and bring your attention to what actually needs to be done, and, more importantly, what's within your control.

Here is an example:

OUTCOME GOAL: Win the game

PROCESS GOALS (Rule of Three):

1. Communicate more
2. Be aggressive in winning possession
3. Take 10 shots on target

By focusing on these controllable actions, you are increasing the chances of the outcome. The intent of the Rule of Three is to remind you of the controllables, to help you focus on the process, and ultimately to help you keep your mind in the present. Take a moment to reflect on a few things that might work for you in your next performance.

VISUALIZE TO ACTUALIZE

Mental imagery, also known as visualization, is accepted by sport psychologists, coaches, and athletes as a very useful psychological skill for mental and physical training. It can also be an effective tool in our goal-setting process. Imagery is the practice of seeing things in our mind's eye. By visualizing getting something done, it creates an image for us to use as a marker. In this way, visualization enhances our objectives. With a concrete image of what our best performance

102

looks like, we are more likely to stay in the challenge-skill sweet spot, since we've mentally rehearsed the actions ahead of time and we are less likely to be surprised during the actual performance. The funny thing is that we all do this subconsciously already, like when we think about what to do on the weekend, or how our life will be in 5 years' time. Imagery is a natural skill that we all have. All that is required is to fine-tune it a bit for greater effectiveness. The more specific and clear our imagery is, the easier it will be to start setting goals. After all, we can't hit a target that we cannot see.

Now, I am not saying that just by visualizing success it will magically happen. All that I am saying is that when we have a clear image of what to do next the more likely we are to follow through.

It is similar to the process of learning to ride a bike or to drive a car. The first tip you give any novice is to tell them to look where they are going, and not down at their hands. With imagery, we essentially pave the road for ourselves metaphorically and neurologically. There is evidence to show that imagery enhances neuromuscular activation, as well as many cognitive processes such as motor control, attention, perception, planning, and memory[30]. When we do visualization, we are training the brain for actual performance.

Next time you are going over your goals, take a moment to visualize the entire process. What will it look like to accomplish this goal? More importantly, what will it *feel* like? Imagery can produce changes in physical performance and in psychological variables that may affect performance.

There are many methods of creating goals, and in reality, it doesn't matter what system you are using as long as you are setting an intention for focusing on things that are within your control. At the end of the day you are the expert of your own life, so use a method that makes sense to you. Customize and adjust until you are consistently reaching your targets. There are bound to be setbacks and struggles along the way but by having a plan written down you are more likely to keep up with it.

Whether it is the 100-Day Plan method or another form of performance planning, the important thing about goals is to set em' and check em'. Don't just write it down somewhere and forget all about it. Goals require constant maintenance, adjustment, and grit. Psychologist Angela Duckworth defines grit as passion and perseverance towards a long-term goal[61]. The more you are clear on these long-term goals, the easier it will be to develop grit and experience flow states more often.

RECAP

- Goal setting has been shown to be beneficial in improving performance, but make sure they are process-oriented rather than outcome-oriented. This is because the process is always within our control as opposed to the outcome which is not.

- The 100-day plan is an effective framework to structure your macro goals into manageable steps.

- Using performance profiling in addition to your goal setting can help develop more awareness of what targets you should set for yourself. It can also be used as a feedback tool.

- The rule of three is a quick micro goal setting technique to implement before a performance or even as a daily reminder.

- Use imagery to visualize what is possible for you. This creates a specific target to work towards and gets you closer to that challenge-skill sweet spot.

6

MINDFULNESS

Overthinking seems to be a national pastime. We are constantly at war with our own thoughts seemingly unable to get a grip. The cause of our suffering tends to lie in the thinking mind, something Zen Buddhism and other traditions have been trying to come to terms with for a few thousand years now. With roots in these ancient practices, meditation has become a way of conditioning the mind to deal with the incessant chatter of waking consciousness: a source of stress, anxiety, and overall suffering for us humans.

By quieting the mind through observation and deliberate attention, as one does with meditation, we reduce our suffering and can learn to be fully present with each momentary experience. As we know, this can optimize our ability to experience flow.

Today practices involving meditation are categorized as *mindfulness.* Dr. Jon Kabatt-Zinn, author of *Full Catastrophe Living,* founder of the mindfulness-based stress reduction (MBSR) program, and pioneer in bringing eastern practices to the west, defines mindfulness as a "non-judgemental present moment awareness"[62]. It doesn't require any incense, candles, or shaving your head, but rather a gentle reminder to bring your attention back to the present whenever your mind wanders.

What was once considered woo-woo spiritual practice is now becoming mainstream, with thousands of peer-reviewed scientific articles highlighting the benefits of mindfulness. These benefits include a reduction in stress, anxiety, depression, aggression, as well as an increase in compassion, productivity, sleep, relationships, and many other benefits.

The practice of mindfulness meditation has also been shown to be associated with relatively reduced activity in the *default mode network (DMN)*[63], a brain network involved in self-related thinking, mind wandering, and excessive rumination. With a reduction in activity in these brain regions, the mind has a greater capacity to focus on the task at hand and is less likely to wander off or get distracted. That is not to say that an increase in the DMN doesn't have its benefits; more activity in the DMN has been shown to be correlated with creativity since there are more neural pathways being connected which link together to create sparks of insight.

However, when it comes to peak performance, we know that *flow follows focus,* and thus it is to our benefit to cultivate mindfulness. Often, the two are thought to be the same thing since they share many similarities, but in actuality, we use mindfulness as a precursor to the flow state. In fact, individuals who go through a mindfulness-based performance enhancement program show significant increases in flow experiences [64].

All of this sounds great, but if it were that easy to do, you wouldn't need a book such as this. Perhaps you have tried mindfulness before but found it impossible to shut off your wandering mind. In this way you have unknowingly realized the truth; it is impossible to shut the mind off voluntarily!

Meditation is not about shutting off our monkey mind but is rather the practice of changing your relationship with thoughts and realizing that they are just that, thoughts. The more we attempt to resist, change, or control these thoughts, the more agitated they become. You can't solve problems created by thinking with *more* thinking. Philosopher Alan Watts puts it best:

"Muddy water is best cleared by leaving it alone."[65]

YOU DON'T HAVE TO BECOME A MONK

You must learn to become a casual observer of thoughts and let them come and go like the clouds in the sky. With time, you realize the mind settles on its own and you have a sense of clarity and space in which to allocate your attention to appropriate matters. The problem lies in the fact that we tend to *react* to external events or internal chatter with a certain degree of avoidance, judgment, or attempt to control or change the experience, and in most cases, it doesn't serve us well. Instead, what we want to create is a bit more space so that we can see things a little more clearly and *respond* to a situation.

An example of this is a baseball pitcher learning how not to get fazed by the negative banter from the crowd or by his own negative inner dialogue and being able to respond with a clear mind rather than reacting with frustration.

To achieve this, we must create a state of mind that will not jump at every little thought but will see it for what it is, just a thought. Some monks, like Matthieu Ricard who serves as the French interpreter for the Dalai Lama, are even able to reduce their physiological responses to unanticipated distractions—like a 115-decibel burst of white noise (equivalent in volume to a gunshot)—by using the skills they've honed through thousands of hours of meditation. When researchers compared his facial muscle response to control groups of non-meditators, they found that while meditating, Ricard had much less facial response than the non-meditators.

Though this study does not mean that by meditating you will become superhuman, it does show that the act of engaging in meditation can possibly temper those reflexive responses that begin in regions of the human nervous system[66]: the response that often gets us into trouble because they are almost automatic. Long-term meditators also produce brain waves in the gamma range, which is the type of brain wave present when novel ideas snap together for the first time: that "a-ha!" moment of insight. Meditation then, has been shown to amplify creativity[67].

It turns out that all of us can produce similar results without thousands of hours of cross-legged cushion time. For example, in 2009, psychologists at the University of North Carolina found that even four days of meditation significantly improved both creativity and cognitive flexibility in test subjects[68]. Rather than devoting decades to becoming a monk, we now know that even a few days of mindfulness can benefit us.

MINDFULNESS MEDITATION

The practice of meditation is not a matter of thinking more clearly about experience, it is the act of experiencing more clearly, including the arising of thoughts themselves. When one thought ends, right before the next thought begins, there is a tiny gap called *now*. Over time we learn to expand that gap until we string enough of them together to elongate the present moment. It is in this space that we have room to do something special. As basketball legend Kobe Bryant once put it:

> *"It's not the number of hours you practice, it's about the number of hours your mind is present during the practice."*

Viktor Frankl, psychologist and holocaust survivor wrote in his book, *Man's Search for Meaning,* that between stimulus and response there is a space, and that in that space is our power to choose our response[69]. This allows us to be more receptive to the nuances of the moment and choose the appropriate course of action. Reacting to a mistake with frustration is completely normal, but it takes our attention away from the task at hand and ultimately moves us away from flow. Instead, the point is to recognize that the feeling of frustration is just an experience, and in most cases is just a distraction. Once we understand this and practice working with our mind's focus through mindfulness, we can quickly shift our attention to engage with what is in front of us regardless of how we are feeling.

We can't necessarily control each thought that pops up in our minds, but we have control over which ones to attend to, and which ones to ignore. Thus, we must train ourselves to use our inner dialogue, or self-talk, as a tool for guiding our minds to the present. Instead of forming the habits of a negative mind, we can move towards a more positive mind. When we hang out in a positive mind long enough, we are better equipped to slip into a state of *no-mind.*

The training of mindfulness allows us to engage our capacity to override a "self-focus", where we are too preoccupied with ourselves and negative focused thinking. What meditation does is help us engage in a "task-focus" instead. In other words, we learn to stop overthinking things and not get too pre-occupied with the self, as well as not getting distracted by task-irrelevant thoughts and sensations. This is not a simple task. Sitting alone with thoughts seems like a nightmare for many people, and it isn't only a modern-day phenomenon. We have always struggled with our internal chatter, as 17th-century philosopher Blaise Pascal puts it:

"All of humanity's problems stem from man's inability to sit quietly in a room alone."

SINGLE POINT MINDFULNESS

When we get pulled by a negative thought, we can choose to respond to it by noticing it, letting it go, and focusing on something else. This type of mindfulness is called single point mindfulness, where we give the mind something specific to focus on, such as the breath, sounds, or physical sensations in order to train attention and lock into the present. The more we train our wandering mind, the easier it becomes to sustain our attention for longer periods of time.

Athletes and other performers can actively practice single point mindfulness to increase their ability to sustain their attention in high-pressure situations. Essentially, practicing mindfulness is like doing bicep curls for your mind. Once you begin the process of focusing on just one thing, after a while you may notice that the internal dust of thought settles, and you find clarity and calmness. In this stillness, you notice certain loops and patterns such as certain thoughts or feelings that keep lingering in consciousness. At first, this may seem unsettling, but as you progress in your training you realize the more you attempt to get rid of these thoughts, the heavier they feel. Therefore, instead of trying to stop or change them, you recognize the thoughts for what they are: just thoughts. Each time we note a thought as a distraction rather than as a story to follow, we train ourselves to be free of our stories and distractions. This creates space for our attention to be fully present and engaged with the here and now.

CONTEMPLATIVE MINDFULNESS

Once we get familiar with single point mindfulness, we can progress to the second type of mindfulness training, which is called contemplative mindfulness. This type of training is a way to objectify thoughts and emotions as something simply in the field of awareness rather than being consumed by it. Here, we can reflect and observe without judgment.

Meditations like this are popular in the Zen tradition where there is no inherent goal, or state to be achieved but rather the point is to "just sit." To someone untrained in this method, it may seem quite silly and unproductive. What good can ever come by sitting and doing nothing? However, it is precisely by sitting and doing nothing that we can begin to understand ourselves and the habitual negative thinking patterns we have paralyzed ourselves with. With this type of meditation, you learn to become a casual observer of your thoughts by objectifying them as something simply in your awareness, and not necessarily meant to define you.

For example, let us say that before a big tryout you are getting anxious and fearful of what might happen. Instead of defining yourself as being anxious or fearful, you can simply observe fear and anxiety as something appearing in your scope of consciousness. By objectifying the thoughts or feelings you are experiencing, you are not held prisoner by them. This allows for more space to respond to the experience with clarity and confidence. By practicing contemplative mindfulness, you are actively training this ability to notice, accept, and let go.

HOW TO MEDITATE

Meditation can come in many forms. All it really takes is paying attention. We can focus our attention through movement, such as feeling and noticing any physical sensations while walking, running, or stretching, or listening attentively to words or music, and even silence. The way we most commonly train in mindfulness though is through mindfulness of the breath.

Some monks take all these forms of meditation to the extreme, such as the marathon monks of Mount Hiei in Japan who complete 1000-day journeys towards enlightenment. Over the span of seven years, the Monks do multiple 100 consecutive days of moving meditation in the form of run/walks spanning 60-kilometers that require 14 to 15 hours to complete. On the seventh and final year of this pilgrimage around Mount Hiei, these monks do a daily 85 kilometers for the first 100 days[70]. That is the equivalent of two Olympic marathons a day for 100 days in a row. These guys redefine the meaning of ultra-endurance athlete!

Of course, you don't need to go to these extreme lengths to harness your focus (or find enlightenment or whatever you're searching for...). Though all you need in order to begin is already within you, it does help to have a system that aids in cultivating the right frame of mind. Thus, when you engage in meditation, I recommend that you follow a three-step procedure to: adjust your body, breathing, and mind.

The Body. The human body is quite the vessel. It does so much for us, so it only makes sense to take good care of it. One needs to have a proper diet, engage in appropriate physical exercise, and avoid forming habits contrary to nurturing a healthy mind-body connection. The mind and body are often viewed as separate, but this is not a correct view: what the body does will directly influence the mind and vice versa. This is because there is no separation between the two: they are one and the same.

Specifically, however, when we talk about the adjustment of the body, we are talking about the seated meditation posture. Keeping a dignified, strong, yet relaxed position is necessary for cultivating a focused body and mind. When you are seated upright, with your back straight, shoulders relaxed, you are essentially telling the body to be present. This is the ideal form of sitting meditation, but in reality, any position will do. It is just easier to pay attention and stay awake when you are upright and in a relaxed yet alert position. Lying down, unfortunately, creates an environment prone to falling asleep, though it does work for some meditation practices such as the body-scan, where one focuses on each muscle group.

The Breath. Let me ask you this: right now, as you are reading, are you breathing?

Congratulations! You just did some mindfulness training. You became aware of something that goes on without you giving it any thought, and that is how we bring awareness and attention to the present moment.

Try this simple exercise next: focus on the breath for just 10 counts, counting each in-breath and out-breath. If you get distracted and lose count, simply start over again at 1. Try it now.

It's not as easy as it seems, right? The mind naturally tends to wander. If you felt like you were able to still your mind enough to count your breaths, try it again for 30 seconds. I'll wait for you to not have a thought.

It is impossible to shut off the mind. The good thing though, is that we don't have to. We need not complicate things when first starting off. Simply learn to follow the breath and notice when you get distracted.

Focusing on the breath does two things for us: (1) it gives the mind something to pay attention to, thus driving the attention to the present, since the breath is always *in* the present, and (2) activates our parasympathetic nervous system, which triggers relaxation, a state that gets our body out of fight or flight mode.

We practice mindfulness first by noticing the moments when we get distracted, and then by guiding our attention to our breathing. As Zen master Thich Nhat Hahn says:

"Conscious breathing is my anchor."[71]

The Mind. At this point, you may feel you are beginning to understand this concept intellectually. But without any previous practice, it is hard to truly understand: you must experience it firsthand. In the context of Zen, the perfection of wisdom and having *no mind* requires *practical experiential* knowledge. In other words: theory without application carries no meaning for someone on the path to mental mastery.

To use a Zen phrase, discussing any conceptual theory is only "*a finger pointing to the moon*": we should not confuse the pointing to the moon as the moon itself. The moon is the actual *experience* of enlightenment and the finger is the attempt to explain or point to the experience. Thus, in Zen training, the emphasis is on direct experience, which we cultivate through meditation.

The minimum amount of practice we need to see actual physiological changes in the brain from practicing mindfulness is around 8 minutes per day. Of course, the more we train the better, but as with most things, it takes time to form a habit. In order to grow and progress we must cultivate both single point and contemplative methods of mindfulness.

Once you have developed a good foundation of the formal mindfulness practice of "just sitting", you will find that you can even bring everyday moments into full awareness. The truth is that we can cultivate mindfulness anywhere we go, no matter where we are, whether we're washing dishes, walking the dog, at the gym, or even a World Cup final.

The following guided mindfulness script can help you experience a blend of the single point focus, and contemplative mindfulness practices. You may have to do it with eyes open at first in order to get a better understanding of the exercise, or you may record the instructions on your phone to listen to (you can also find a guided meditation on my website: www.flowperformancepsych.com). No need to rush anything, follow along at your own pace. Set aside 5-10 minutes in a quiet environment where you will not be distracted.

Exercise: Guided Meditation

Please find a comfortable sitting position. Notice the position of your feet, arms, and hands. Allow your eyes to close gently. **Pause for 10 seconds.**

Now breathe in and out gently and deeply several times. Notice the sound and sensations of your own breath as you breathe in and out. **Pause for 10 seconds.**

Continue to follow the breath, noticing its natural rhythm. If you get distracted by a thought, simply guide your attention back to the breath without any judgment.

Now, with your eyes still closed, if that feels comfortable: focus your attention on your surroundings. Notice any sounds that may be occurring. Notice any sounds that may be occurring both inside and outside the room. Don't try to label the sounds, just simply continue to notice them. **Pause for 10 seconds.**

Focus your attention on the areas where your body touches the chair, mat, or cushion on which you are sitting. Focus on your back, your arms, your hands, your buttocks, your thighs, and your feet. **Pause for 10 seconds.**

Now pay attention to the sensations in the rest of your body and observe how they may change over time without any effort on your part. Don't try to alter these sensations, just notice them as they occur. **Pause for 10 seconds.**

Turn your focus to the inner chatter of your mind. See if you can notice any doubts or other thoughts without doing anything but noticing them. Just watch your reservations, concerns, and worries as though they are elements of a parade passing through your mind. **Pause for 10 seconds.**

See if you can simply notice them and acknowledge their presence. **Pause for 10 seconds.** Don't try to make them go away or change them in any way. **Pause for 10 seconds.**

As the session comes to a close, allow your mind to drift. No need to give it any particular instruction. If it wants to think, let it think. **Pause for 15 seconds.**

And finally, slowly let yourself once again tune into your surroundings. **Pause for 10 seconds.** Notice any sounds, smells, and any physical sensations of your body. **Pause for 10 seconds.** Once again notice your own breathing. **Pause for 10 seconds.**

And when you are ready, open your eyes. Give yourself a moment to notice how you feel in the present moment.

* * *

THE OODA LOOP

The more we practice intentionally paying attention to what we're doing on a regular basis, the more present we will be, and as a result, the more able we will be to perform at our very best. This is even more crucial in environments that require us to cope with heavy demands on our attention or our bodies, such as high-performance sport.

But to get the most out of our minds and bodies, we don't need just a theoretical notion: we require a mental model of looking at and understanding the unfolding world around us.

Life and performance are full of ambiguity and uncertainty; it can be challenging to shift perspectives and use multiple tools and methods in order to navigate its complexity and reach our goals. We often get caught up in the idea of how the world *should* be, rather than focusing on *what is*.

Military strategist Colonel John Boyd created a mental model that does precisely this. He revolutionized the methods of every air force in the world by developing the concept of the OODA-Loop, which stands for Observe, Orient, Decide, and Act[72].

Although first developed as a military strategy for the US Air Force back in the '70s, it has since been applied to business, sports, and other domains to guide an otherwise stressed mind in chaotic circumstances. It provides us with a mental checklist to help us move forward with the best course of action in any situation.

Although the actual strategy involves a complex interplay of feedback loops, data input, and other variables that are crucial for larger systems like running a military operation, we can apply the OODA-Loop to our own individual lives. Let's briefly go over the stages, and then I'll explain how OODA relates to mindfulness and flow.

Observe

During the first stage, we need to be attentive and alert, observing the environment. We gather what input and data we can by noticing the unfolding circumstances and information available to us. A fighter pilot, for example, needs to be paying attention to environmental cues and to be scanning the skies for any enemies. And a goalkeeper needs to remain attentive by constantly watching for potential counterattacks by opposing players.

Orient

Once something changes in the environment (internal or external) we must analyze the information, compare it to previous experiences, and then deduct the relevant cues to create a new mental system. Orientation isn't just a state you're in; it's a process. Our brains are always orienting, but we can train them to be more efficient in weeding out what's relevant and what's not. The more quickly we can do this, the more quickly we can reach our intended targets in the moment.

The pilot in the example above must quickly readjust her position if she notices that an enemy plane is right behind her. And the goalkeeper will need to do a quick check behind him to orient himself in relation to the net whenever his team loses possession. In both examples, having a preconceived mental checklist of what to do when in these situations, reduces the mental friction about what to do next.

Decide

The next step is deciding what to do once we have observed the situation and oriented ourselves. The athletes who decide what to do most quickly tend to outperform the ones who are slower to decide, especially in high-pressure situations.

A person who has achieved mastery in a specific domain is able to quickly notice when the situation lines up with a specific pre-conceived plan and can then execute that mental model without having to make a conscious decision. They just act. This is effortless effort: a stage of mastery where the action becomes unconscious.

If our fighter pilot hesitates, or if the other pilot decides what to do more quickly, then the battle is lost. And the goalkeeper must decide quickly to dive left when a player's body position suggests they will shoot in that direction in order to have a better chance of saving it.

Act

The variables in any given situation are infinite so you must trust yourself to move with the play, rather than against it. It takes a while to get to this level, though. This is why training is so important: it smoothes out the decision process through repetition so we can access the right actions without having to spend the time or effort to think about the right thing to do. When you act without thinking you have a mind without mind. You get out of your own way and just do it.

For example, I always struggled with making decisions in my life, regardless of how big or small. I decided to start with the little things such as quickly deciding what to order at a restaurant. The more I reduced hesitation, the quicker my actions became.

THE 3 A's OF MINDFULNESS

The OODA-Loop is an effective mental model to help elite performers navigate complex and ambiguous situations. But we can simplify this even further and apply a more mindful approach that I developed called the 3 A's of Mindfulness. The 3 A's are a simplified version of OODA that creates a quick internal feedback system that allows you to stay calm and present during moments of distress and is much easier to remember. The 3 A's stand for *Awareness, Acceptance, and Action*.

Awareness

Just like the *observe* and *orient* stages of OODA, the first step is to just simply become aware of what is going on. In particular, notice your present moment state of mind. Are you tense, nervous, relaxed, happy, or angry? How does the body feel? Is your mind busy or quiet? Just bring whatever you are feeling into awareness, without getting caught up in judgment. A useful technique to use is an "internal thermometer", internally gauging your experience from 1-10 (1 being bored, 10 being extremely anxious). Or, if you prefer, you may use a color system: Are you feeling *red* (tense, nervous, results-oriented, over-aggressive, etc.) or *blue* (calm, focused, present, process-focused, etc.)?

Take a moment now to simply check in with yourself. Reading this book, how do you feel? Don't label anything as good or bad, just observe and become aware of what is happening around you, and how you are feeling in relation to it. It doesn't matter what you are feeling, just simply bring it into frame of mind. Once we have done this, we move into...

Acceptance

Now that you are aware of what you are experiencing, allow yourself to accept whatever you may be feeling, positive OR negative. Remember, mindfulness is the practice of non-judgmental present moment awareness, which means that regardless of the state you are in you are simply observing it with curiosity without putting a label on the experience. This is just one moment of many, so don't fall into the trap of attaching yourself to it.

This stage is where self-talk techniques such as cognitive reframing are useful. Instead of correlating feeling nervous with a bad performance, you can instead say "It's OK to be nervous. It just means I am ready to perform." Or, view whatever you are feeling as an experience rather than something that defines you; "I am just *experiencing* anxiety/fear/anger in this moment" is more helpful than "I am an anxious/fearful/angry person."

If you feel a bit sluggish, or nervous before competing, learn to simply accept it for what it is: just an experience. What can also be helpful is viewing anxiety as a friend whom you welcome with open arms. This way, you objectify the emotion or thought, and it has less power over you. This is exemplified in the poem *The Guest House,* by Rumi:

This being human is a guest house. Every morning a new arrival.

A joy, a depression, a meanness, some momentary awareness comes as an unexpected visitor.

Welcome and entertain them all!...

The dark thought, the shame, the malice, meet them at the door laughing, and invite them in.

Be grateful whoever comes, because each has been sent as a guide from beyond.[73]

You have the power to *decide* what to do in situations of stress. Accept the chaos and invite your inner demons to tea. By letting go of control it lowers tension and creates more space in which to take...

Action

Once you have become aware of the present moment state and accept whatever you are feeling, you may start to course-correct if necessary. As in the OODA-Loop, we need to take action to make sure we end up in a favourable position. The Action step is where you do the things that work for you in order to relax, refocus or readjust, if necessary, to accomplish what you want to accomplish. If you find yourself way above your normal level (your baseline) for anxiety, for example, perhaps do some breathing to bring arousal down and use self-talk to lock-in.

What is your action piece? How can you shift your attention with a specific *action* in order to focus on the task at hand?

The next time you find yourself in a high-pressure moment (or any moment for that matter), remember to use the 3 A's like a mental checklist to bring mind and body together. It is a simple process to follow that can be the difference between performing with presence or being absent-minded.

Exercise: Create a 3 A's framework

What does your 3 A's framework look like? Using the worksheet provided, write down step-by-step what you will do in a stressful situation. For instance, you might write:

Awareness – Stop for 15 seconds and notice what I'm sensing and experiencing.

Acceptance – Accept my anxiety as just a passing event.

Action – Reframe anxiety as positive with self-talk and then focus on my breath.

* * *

TACTICAL BREATHING

Most people are not trained in actionable steps to help them bring their attention back or to lower their arousal when they're distracted or upset. It is a difficult thing to do, but there are some simple and effective techniques that can help get you started. Breath training is one of these actions that can be very easily and readily applied to any situation.

Breathing is both an involuntary process, meaning we don't have to think about it for it to happen, and a voluntary process, which means we have full control of it as well. Breathing is at the foundation of any mindfulness practice since the breath can be taken wherever you go, and as such we have access to it whenever we want. As Eugen Herrigel says in *Zen in the Art of Archery:*

"The more one concentrates on breathing, the more the external stimuli fade into the background... In due course, one even grows immune to larger stimuli, and at the same time detachment from them becomes easier and quicker. Care has only to be taken that the body is relaxed whether standing, sitting or lying, and if one then concentrates on breathing one soon feels oneself shut in by impermeable layers of silence. One only knows and feels that one breathes. And, to detach oneself from this feeling and knowing, no fresh decision is required, for the breathing slows down of its own accord, becomes more and more economical in the use of breath, and finally, slipping by degrees into a blurred monotone, escapes one's attention altogether."[74]

Focusing on the breath is one of the most effective ways to not only help you pay attention but also has the added benefit of lowering physiological arousal. Navy SEALs know this very well (the military seems to be a breeding ground for high-performance techniques due to its emphasis on staying alive). They implement *tactical breathing* as a strategy for when the going gets tough. In particular, *box breathing* is very effective in reducing heart rate, lowering cortisol levels, and activating the *parasympathetic* nervous system, or in other words, your relaxation response.

Box breathing goes something like this: inhale for a count of 4 (can be longer as you progress), hold the breath for a count of 4, exhale for 4, and then hold for another 4. A few sets of this can help regulate mind and body. If you have a heart rate monitor, you can experiment with this yourself. After a tough workout see how quickly your heart rate goes down after doing some box breaths.

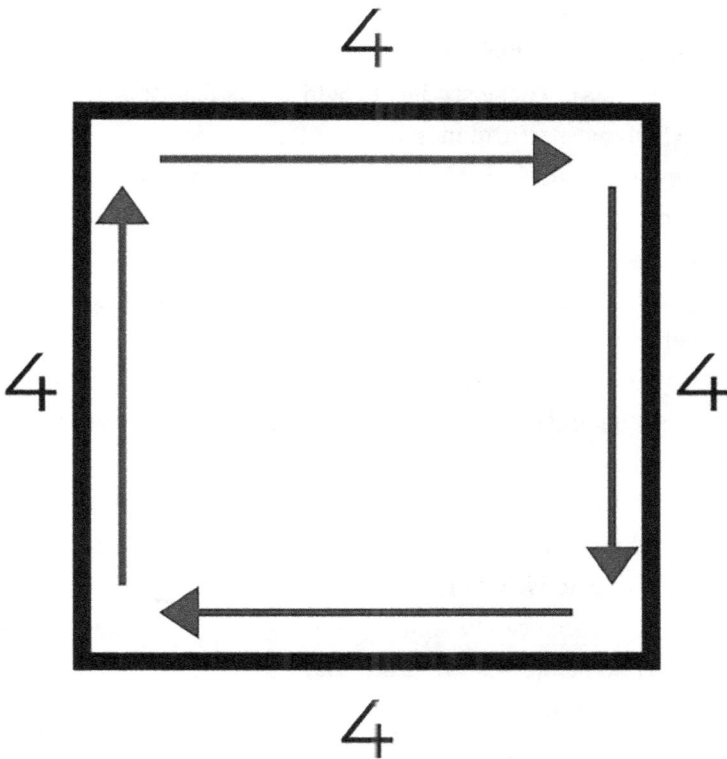

DO WE THINK FIRST, OR FEEL FIRST?

Research shows the benefits of having a more mindful approach to our performance. In my own athletic career, I always noticed that the more I thought about my performance during the actual game, the worse it turned out. One study in particular showed that golfers who underwent brain scans while performing a putting task performed more poorly when the verbal-linguistic center of the brain was showing activation[75]. What this means is that the golfers who had more cognitive activity did worse than those who didn't. Furthermore, in flow we experience transient hypofrontality: the temporal deactivation of the pre-frontal cortex (which houses most of our cognitive functions such as self-analysis). These studies provide evidence that thinking less tends to increase performance.

How we think and feel affects the way we perform. But too often we add layers of excessive thinking to how we are feeling. For example, when we are stressed out, we may ask "why am I stressed?." In itself a very good introspective question. But we tend to fall into the "think first, feel second" trap.

Often, we experience what filmmaker, futurist, and philosopher Jason Silva calls *temporal dislocation*: our mind is not present in the location we are physically in!

We get caught up in either the past or the future and don't experience whatever is happening now. Our mind has shifted away from the present and is disconnected from our bodies.

This happens because the source of our stress lies in either something that happened prior, or something that has not yet occurred, both of which we can do nothing about. In order to effectively deal with the stress, we must become familiar with it.

Instead of asking "why am I stressed?", you might say, "I am experiencing stress." Experience whatever is present and do not try to label the experience as positive or negative. Sometimes stress is necessary for us and can lead to some positive change. Don't get lost in the past or the future about the answer to a particular problem because you must first come to terms with what is currently happening. When we feel an emotion that causes stress, such as anger, anxiety, or fear, we can let that emotion run its course and then cope with the stressful situation in whatever way will help us. Only then can we comprehend what the emotion was trying to tell us. When we're in the heat of our emotions, they have a way of very easily leading us to catastrophize a situation.

After we have dealt with the experience of the emotion, we can start to course correct and implement cognitive strategies.

A useful analogy that is used in psychology is the story of the elephant and the rider, which is credited to Jonathan Haidt[76]. The elephant represents the emotional mind, and the rider represents the thinking, rational mind. Sometimes the elephant is unpredictable and acts out. The rider can't control the elephant completely, so they have to learn to direct the elephant and calm it down by allowing it the space it needs. Thus, by relinquishing some control, the rider gets control back.

In the same way, our thoughts can deal with our emotions, but only when we learn to ride out our emotional unpredictability and see them as temporary bumps on our road to mastery. Mindfulness teaches us to see our present moment experiences more objectively and be completely OK with them. Now, this is a superpower any athlete would benefit from.

Meditation isn't fundamentally about the breath, and it isn't about *thinking* about the present moment. Meditation is merely being fully engaged with the very act of doing what we're doing. So then, you may wonder, what is the point of meditation practices where we just sit and don't do anything? This method of practice is about training your attention. The mind is a muscle, and meditation is the weight your mind is lifting in order to control and direct attention with intention. Sitting around doing nothing, otherwise known as our default state, is when our minds are most inclined to wander, and therefore it's during these times that it's hardest to keep your attention on the task. This is why we practice: to make sure we can *experience* what we are doing, rather than just thinking about it along with our hundreds of other thoughts and distractions. Mind without mind.

Once we've decoupled our emotions from our thinking mind and decided that just because something makes us feel a certain way doesn't mean we need to identify with that particular emotion, it opens us up to a wider perspective in which to operate. As 4th-century Chinese philosopher Zhuang Zhoi (also rendered as Chuang Tzu) writes:

> *"The perfect man employs his mind as a mirror – it grasps nothing, yet it refuses nothing; it receives, but does not keep."*

Mindfulness is the gateway to flow state. All it takes is to begin. There are many great meditation apps such as Headspace, Calm, or Waking Up by Sam Harris that are a great place to learn meditation. Alternatively, you may visit my website (www.flowperformancepsych.com) for guided meditations and other mindfulness resources.

Each moment is another opportunity for mindfulness. Start with just focusing on ten breaths when you wake up. Then progress to sitting for five minutes, and then increasing that to ten minutes. It will be difficult at first, but once you have formed the habit it will become second nature to you. Remember to be compassionate to yourself; there is no one perfect way of meditating. As headspace co-founder and Buddhist monk Andy Puddicombe says:

> *"There is no good or bad meditation. Only awareness, and non-awareness."*

RECAP

· Flow follows focus, and the way we train focus is through mindfulness.

· Mindfulness is defined as a present moment, non-judgmental awareness. It is a type of systematic mental training that expands self-awareness and self-regulation. Practicing mindfulness has been shown to quiet down our Default Mode Network which is the normal busy state of mind.

- The 3 A's (awareness, acceptance, action) can be used as a guide in high-stress environments and situations. It acts as an emergency action plan of sorts which with practice becomes second nature.

- Breath training is foundational to mindfulness. Practice following the breath throughout the day and incorporate techniques such as box breathing to activate your body's parasympathetic (relaxation) response.

- Apps such as *Headspace, Calm*, and *Waking Up (Sam Harris)* are great resources for getting into meditation.

7

GROUP FLOW

In addition to the individual experience, flow can also occur within groups of people that pursue challenges together in what is known as *group flow*. Individual flow is enjoyable, but humans are social creatures, so naturally, we find group activities even more pleasurable[77]. French Sociologist Émile Durkheim coined the term *collective effervescence* to mean a moment when a community or society come together to simultaneously communicate the same thought and participate in the same action. Such moments bond individuals and serve to unify the group[78].

This can occur in teams where everything seems to click and each member acts in sync, as if one organism. Bill Russel, former center for the Boston Celtics, once spoke about this near-spiritual experience:

> *"Every so often a Celtic game would heat up so that it became more than a physical or even mental game and would be magical. That feeling is difficult to describe, and I certainly never talked about it when I was playing. When it happened, I could feel my play rise to a new level.... The game would just take off, and there'd be a natural ebb and flow that reminded you of how*

rhythmic and musical basketball is supposed to be.... It was almost as if we were playing in slow motion."

Humans are social beings. Many of us thrive from collaboration with others. Creative collaborations and meetings are essential for companies like Google or Patagonia. Jazz groups rely on the improvisation and challenging of its members to create their masterpieces. It even occurs in operating rooms:

"Surgeons say that during a difficult operation they have the sensation that the entire operating team is a single organism, moved by the same purpose; they describe it as a 'ballet' in which the individual is subordinated to the group performance, and all involved share in the feeling of harmony and power."[79]

Of course, having more individuals involved with a task increases its complexity. Controlling the conditions for one person is difficult as it is. But it is this increase in challenge that provides a unique environment for flow to occur at a more profound level. For example, in a study of over 300 professionals at three different companies, researchers discovered that the people who participated in group flow were the highest performers[80]. It is the ultimate human experience to share common objectives and tackle problems together.

At the individual level, we can experience micro and macro flow as discussed in earlier chapters, but if we zoom out, we can see a broader picture. I believe that flow experience exists on a spectrum, with individual-level flow on one end, and group flow on the other. Social flow may be an experience where an individual is in a group setting and experiences flow due to the social factors involved, such as communication and interaction with others, but the corresponding level of flow has not reached a collective level within the group.

An individual can move from one end to another throughout a performance and is also dependent on other members of the team, who are also adding or subtracting to the collective level of group flow.

By understanding flow in this way, we can increase the potential for effective team performance. Let's discuss how you can maximize the probability of moving from individual flow to a collective group flow experience.

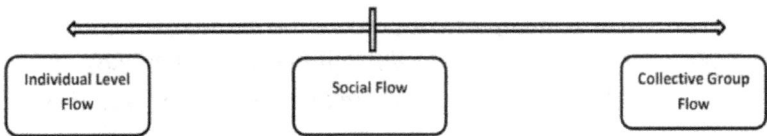

| Individual Level Flow | Social Flow | Collective Group Flow |

THE CONDITIONS OF GROUP FLOW

Dr. Keith Sawyer, a former student of Csikszentmihalyi's and one of the world's leading scientific experts on creativity, innovation, and learning, as well as the author of *Group Genius*, builds upon Csikszentmihalyi's characteristics of individual flow and describes group flow as a peak experience, a group performing at its top level of ability. Interestingly, Sawyer drew a lot of inspiration and research from Jazz musicians and improv theatre groups. In these free-flowing arenas, individuals build off of each other's response to produce something truly unique and amazing.

But these groups don't just hope for the best on any given performance; they are actually following certain rules and conditions that harness their ability. They believe that creativity is a state to be trained, and not a static trait that someone does or does not have.

Dr. Sawyer outlines 10 conditions for group flow that builds upon Csikszentmihalyi's conditions for individual flow[81]. They are:

1. **Shared clear goals** - Similar to having a clear objective in individual flow, having a shared goal can harness a team's focus on the task at hand. When everyone is on the same page about the objective, team-mates don't waste time discussing what needs to be done. Everyone already knows where they have to be, and what they have to do.

2. **Close Listening** - Listening, being heard, and following up on what has been said helps drive attention to the now and ultimately increases performance. When teammates take the time to be completely present with one another, trust begins to build. If I know you are willing to listen to me, then I am more likely to do the same with you. People who listen closely are energizing and propel others around them to new heights. Lend an ear to a teammate and see what happens!

3. **Complete Concentration** - Just as individuals need to have a deep focus, this needs to span to the collective as well. A lack of focus creates a lack of greatness. It is one of the reasons why achieving a state of group flow is so difficult because if even one person drifts off for too long it can have big consequences on the outcome. Think of how many teams blow a lead in the dying moments of a game because of a lack of focus.

4. **Being in control** - Group flow increases when people feel their primary needs are being met. According to self-determination theory, these needs are *autonomy, relatedness, and competence.* Allowing individuals the freedom to make choices gives them a sense of control. Couple this with a sense of unity and relatedness as well as providing the right feedback to make them feel competent, and you have a recipe for success.

5. **Blending egos** - Each person's ideas build on those contributed by

his or her teammates. A team needs to cultivate a culture of competing with one another, rather than competing against one another. When you compete *against* one another, you create an environment where people are afraid of making mistakes. When you compete *with* one another you are running towards your shared objectives and not away from failure. When it's OK to make mistakes, it allows space for you and your teammates to compete to be better versions of yourselves. Plus, it creates a sense of psychological safety which has been shown to be a predictor of team success[82].

6. **Equal participation** – In a successful team, everyone gets a chance to be a leader and contribute. As the saying goes, "a rising tide lifts all boats." Of course, some key members will play a more active role in contributing to the task at hand, but allowing the less influential players an opportunity to step up to bat every once in a while, will help overall team cohesion. Each member needs to know and accept their role on the team and to feel that their role is important. Even a small role like being a vocal and positive bench player can contribute to the larger picture. Good leaders will understand and reinforce the idea that no one on their team will be left out or made to feel like they are not a part of the bigger picture. However, when it comes to higher levels of competition, this tends to be most effective when group members are highly skilled and already have a foundation of competence.

7. **Familiarity** – Research shows that the more familiar a group is with each other the better they perform. This is because trust is developed through shared experiences. However, this relationship is only beneficial up to a point: when a group becomes *too* familiar, they lose the drive to change things up and challenge themselves. This is why it is so hard to create a dynasty of consistent success. It requires constant maintenance and the occasional change in personnel.

8. **Good communication** - External feedback is hard to come by, but when it is immediate, positive, and clear, a team can effectively move towards the completion of a task. The desire for communication is hard-wired into us. We are social beings after all. It is the way we share ideas and let others know what we think and feel. The better the communication in a team, the faster the transmission of information, which leaves less room for ambiguity about what needs to be done. Good communication and shared objectives go hand-in-hand.

9. **Potential for failure** - Risk heightens our attention to the present moment and this is amplified when there is more collective risk. Letting yourself down is one thing, but, on a team, letting *others* down has a much greater consequence. With this greater risk comes a certain responsibility and assertiveness becomes even more necessary.

Think of a World Cup final: your team is down one goal and it is the 90th minute. The stakes are high, and you can bet the losing team is focused on just one thing: scoring a goal. But of course, this depends on the perceived level of challenge compared to skill level. Too much challenge and perceived risk can result in debilitating anxiety.

10. **Always say "yes, and"** - The goal is to gather momentum. When an improv group member starts a scene with "Hey, there's a blue elephant in the bathroom,", responding "No there's not," is not going to further enhance the scene. "Yeah, sorry, there was no more space in the closet," makes it go somewhere really interesting! Moving the activity forward allows for greater potential and possibilities. A successful team with a focus on everyone's efforts contributes to getting the team to its ultimate goal.

When a teammate speaks out in a meeting and suggests a potential solution to a problem, as a teammate or leader, make sure you then build upon this idea. For example, say someone suggests that everyone come to training at least 15 minutes early. Instead of responding that this won't work, a response that builds on that idea might be: "Yes, and let's create a group chat to let the team know if you are running late." By listening to one another and by building on one another's ideas, the team experiences more psychological safety, and the stage is set for achieving shared objectives.

Within these elements, we can also see where the environmental triggers for flow show up. If you remember, the environmental conditions we've identified that make it more likely to experience flow are novelty, unpredictability, complexity, and pattern recognition. If cultivated in the right way, these conditions can amplify a team's performance.

For example, cultivating familiarity within a team creates a sense of pattern recognition. Unpredictability and complexity naturally arise when you put a group of people together, and this eventually breeds novelty since new challenges continually arise. Be sure to look for these triggers within the environment you are in and use them to your advantage.

TASK VERSUS SOCIAL COHESION

Fostering a group environment that embodies these conditions is a recipe for success. Group flow has been shown to be more frequent in highly cohesive teams in which there is an agreement on goals, procedures, roles, and patterns of interpersonal relations, and the team's competence is high. When there is an agreement, teams tend to be more cohesive, and group flow is more frequent[83].

Cohesion is defined as a "dynamic process that is reflected in the tendency of a group to stick together and remain united in the pursuit of its instrumental objectives and/or for the satisfaction of member affective needs"[84]. In other words, cohesion can be categorized into two groups: task cohesion, how the group tends to focus on a goal and performance - and social cohesion - the degree to which the group enjoys each other's company outside of the performance context, such as going out together and forming friendships.

It is difficult to determine the direction of the cohesion and performance relationship, as teams might perform better because they are cohesive, or they might be more cohesive because of good performances. A meta-analysis of the research on group cohesion done at the United States Army Research Institute for the Behavioral and Social Sciences found that the stronger direction of effect seems to be from performance to cohesiveness, rather than from cohesiveness to performance. However, the researchers noted that this doesn't mean that cohesion-performance doesn't exist, it just means it seems to have a smaller effect. Changes in cohesiveness brought about by good performance are likely to have a stronger effect than the changes in performance that occur by team social cohesiveness[85].

During my graduate studies, I had an opportunity to explore this relationship as it relates to flow. In my research, I wanted to see what type of group cohesion—task or social—had a greater effect on the individual experience of flow within team sports. I asked 87 athletes from 5 different teams in various sports to complete an assessment of their perception of group cohesion within the team using the Group Environment Questionnaire (GEQ)[86], and then measured their experiences of flow after a training session on three separate occasions using the Flow Short Scale (FSS)[87].

The results showed that social cohesion (the amount to which a group enjoys each other's company) has a more significant influence on the level of flow experienced in individuals in a group setting over task cohesion (how well a team gets along in pursuit of a common objective). This is a novel idea, but in-line with the theoretical framework of group cohesion, in particular, that cohesiveness breeds positive performance[88]. This challenges the idea proposed by other studies that claim group performance is not enhanced by fostering interpersonal attraction.

Regardless of which side of the argument you are on, it seems most likely that members of cohesive groups exert more effort towards successful task performance for the intrinsic pleasure of completing a task. Things are just more fun when we do them together. Although we don't necessarily need to like each other to get it done, it sure doesn't hurt to play alongside someone you care for. If we take a look at the greatest dynasty teams in past sporting history: the Chicago Bulls in the '90s, the Edmonton Oilers in the late '80s, and Liverpool F.C. in the '70s/'80s for example, they all had high task cohesion of course, but what really made them a *dynasty* was their social cohesion. They were all a tight-knit group who would go above and beyond for each other. Therefore, it is equally important to take care of the "human" side of the sports business.

HOW TO CREATE COHESION

The question naturally arises then, of how we can increase team cohesion. Just as we do mental training on an individual level, teams and groups can benefit from following the Mental Performance Training (MPT) framework to increase their cohesiveness. Performing more consistently in the zone is an enjoyable experience for any individual athlete but creating the right conditions for a group of individuals to feel and perform at their very best is even more so.

Achieving flow state on your own is difficult enough as it is, and adding more people to the mix can make things even harder to navigate; but group flow does create a greater sense of achievement and satisfaction than going at it alone. In fact, teams that have higher interdependent tasks (that is, tasks that involve cooperation with and the involvement of others) have been shown to experience group flow more frequently[89]. What this means is that sports such as soccer, football, basketball, or handball, which have higher interdependence tasks, will report more social flow than sports or activities with lower interdependence tasks such as cricket. Adding more people to the mix increases challenge because there are tasks that require the group members to act harmoniously together.

But how can sports teams create an environment that can foster this type of performance? To understand this better, we must look deeper into the mechanisms of successful group collaboration. Studies comparing "solitary flow" to "interactive flow" showed that the more social an activity, the higher "flow enjoyment" was for the participants. This means that we enjoy flow more when we are in a group. We know that higher enjoyment leads to higher motivation, which ultimately can fuel great performance. However, it is crucial that each individual understands that they are responsible for their own motivation and clarify the reasons for why they are there. Motivation must come from within, and only then it can be used to enhance group cohesion.

To establish conditions in which individuals feel safe sharing their motivations, the team must foster greater self-awareness and greater role clarity. Therefore, to create an environment conducive to flow, the group must cultivate a self-leadership type of environment where everyone is allowed to contribute their expertise at any given time. This way, leadership is a flowing process that does not designate one specific leader but allows the collective contribution of certain individuals at specific times in which they feel they have great competence because of the self-efficacy established in creating a self-motivated environment.

For example, instead of a top-down driven process to address players missing training, decided by the coach or management, the players themselves can be given the power to decide what the penalties will be for missing training. This way, the players are held accountable by themselves, and thus more likely to adhere to the rules.

USING MPT FOR GROUP FLOW

Group collaboration starts with the individual, but it is the collective contribution of individuals on the same page that fuels performance. Creating the right conditions for a team to perform well together involves many variables and cannot be summarized neatly in a step-by-step process. Nonetheless, we may apply the elements of our Mental Performance Training (MPT) model of self-awareness, clear objectives, and mindfulness to increase team cohesion, and ultimately performance.

If you are involved in any team sports as an athlete or coach, then you may apply this training to your team members. Even if you are not involved in a team sport, there are always social elements and a group of people that you may consider your team. As an athlete, it's important to be aware of the dynamics of collective cohesion even if you don't necessarily have control over the environment. If you are a coach or manager, creating the right conditions for flow within your environment is a way to ensure your team is maximizing their potential.

Keeping in mind the ten conditions of group flow outlined earlier, you may start to see how each element of Mental Performance Training ties into it. The more of these conditions you create, the greater likelihood of group flow. Under which conditions do you see self-awareness, mindfulness, and clear objectives fit in? There is a lot of overlap between them, but by focusing on the three core ideas of MPT, we can actively train team members to act as one organism.

Let's start with self-awareness, and how we can apply psychological techniques to develop a more cohesive team.

Self (Collective) Awareness

Individuals who take the time for introspection and a greater sense of self-understanding will ultimately have a clearer path. Teams are no different in their pursuits, except that it is difficult to get everyone on the same page. However, by spending some time to uncover collective norms and values, we can get team members to buy into a purpose that is bigger than themselves.

The first step then, is to become aware of a team's social structure: are people getting along? Where are some of the problem areas? Could you find ways to increase social cohesion such as having more opportunities for everyone to get together? Is there something I could be doing better or more effectively?

Usually, at the start of a new season, for example, team members are fairly new, and cohesion hasn't had the chance to form. Having more team outings can start to shape relationships and you will find individuals organically forming a bond. This way you can harness novelty and turn it into pattern recognition. Of course, not everyone will get along (unpredictability); instead of seeing this as a bad thing, understand that this is a normal process and that creating a more intentional approach to navigating this complexity can help move a team forward in developing cohesion.

Conflict is a good thing: it creates forward momentum. Teams should sit down with the intention of hashing out issues and developing a team philosophy and culture. Allowing equal participation, close listening, and an "always say yes, and" mindset during team meetings can help bring ideas and barriers to the surface.

In order to tackle issues that may get in the way of group performance and flow, we must first become aware of those issues. This exercise is similar to the one individuals can do, it just involves a more complex interplay of ideas. As a group, sit down and have a discussion around what barriers are currently holding everyone back. Allow everyone to have a voice and leave the analysis for after each member has had an opportunity to speak.

One method I find useful is to have everyone write down one or more issues they currently have as a member of the team. Then draw the pieces of paper out of a hat or box anonymously. This way the issue is addressed without pointing fingers at any one individual. We are attacking the barriers, not the person. Once barriers are brought up, the group can decide how to tackle them. For example, making sure everyone shows up for practice is important, and is an issue we can solve by setting group norms and values. But perhaps making the playoffs is an unrealistic goal for the time being and the outcome is not so much within our control since there are other teams that are in a better position to reach that target. To help sort out these obstacles it is crucial to decipher which of the issues are important, and which ones are within the group's control.

	IMPORTANT	NOT IMPORTANT
WITHIN OUR CONTROL	Our own efforts and communication	Focusing on other teams
OUT OF OUR CONTROL	How well other teams perform	Negative comments about us

Team Exercise: Sort out the team's obstacles

As a team, go through all the variables within the team's control and decide which ones are important and worth paying attention to. Allow for open communication and psychological safety.

Tip: For coaches, it is important to consider the impact you are having on your athletes. Are you challenging them too much, or too little? Rather than thinking of mental resilience as a fixed trait, look at resilience as a capacity that can be developed over time in the context of athlete- environment interactions. This means your role as a coach is to not only challenge athletes to become better, but also to support them. Challenge involves having high expectations and helps to instill accountability and responsibility. Support means enabling people to develop their personal qualities and helps promote learning and to build trust. Researchers David Fletcher and Mustafa Sarkar created a challenge-support matrix for developing mental resilience[90]:

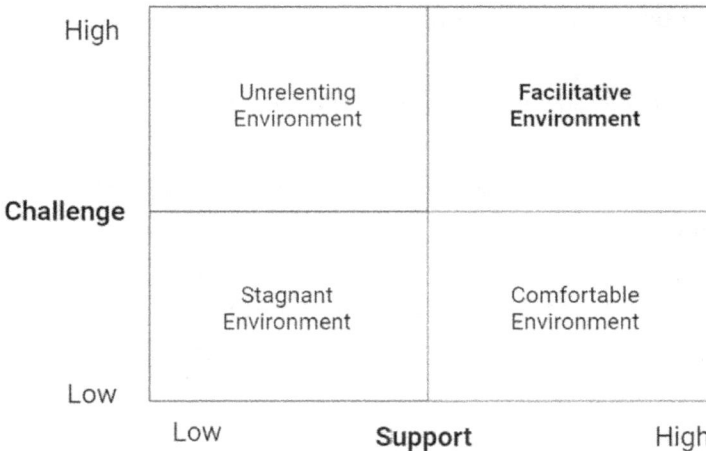

	Low Support	High Support
High Challenge	Unrelenting Environment	**Facilitative Environment**
Low Challenge	Stagnant Environment	Comfortable Environment

The ideal environment would be a facilitative environment where there is high challenge, but also high support. Making sure you are not over or under challenging/supporting your athletes is a crucial skill to master in order to promote group flow. Remember, one of the most important conditions for flow is the balance between challenge and skill. In the team discussions, include some space for feedback on whether the athletes feel adequately challenged and supported.

* * *

Once you have brought barriers to the surface, the next step is to define what it means to be this particular group in this particular moment in time. Just because something has worked in the past does not mean it will work this time around. There are so many variables that affect cohesion and performance. Just one new team member can drastically change the team's dynamic for better or for worse, so it is of utmost importance to regularly review team norms and values so that it matches the current moment. Here are a few questions to dissect with your team to start the process of self and group awareness:

- What are our current strengths? Weaknesses?
- What does it mean to be "us"?
- What are some of our core values? Does everyone agree with them?
- How do we handle setbacks?
- What is our process for dealing with negative behaviour?
- Do we lack task cohesion or social cohesion?
- What kind of culture do we want to build? What will our legacy be?
- What is our definition of success?

Great teams are never created out of thin air. It takes a lot of buy-in, patience, constant reflection, and evaluation to reach success. But by spending time on becoming more aware of its members, a team is in a better position to reach success because they have clearly defined what it means.

Team Exercise: Create a team philosophy

After you have gone over barriers and understood what is within your control, sit down as a team and define your MPP (Mission, Purpose, Philosophy) that was introduced in the Self-Awareness chapter. Have it somewhere visible, and make sure the collective language you use in the team on a daily basis reflects your MPP.

* * *

CLEAR OBJECTIVES

Unclear objectives are one of the biggest barriers to a group's performance. Once the group is aware of any potential barriers and has defined an identity (or actively working towards it), the stage is set for everyone to be on board towards a common goal. Teams should spend time getting clear on what their targets are and ensure that the majority of the group agrees with its direction. Some disagreement is necessary; too much familiarity creates stagnation and having someone push against the grain propels the group in new directions.

For example, if most of the team agrees that a top 5 finish is achievable, but one or two members believe that a top 3 is doable, then it might motivate the group to push harder. As long as the core values of the group are shared and each individual understands their role and accepts it, great things are likely to happen.

Naturally, as we progress through becoming aware of norms and values, a team gets closer to agreeing upon a certain objective. It is important that the group itself sets goals for themselves that are realistic and meaningful to that particular group of individuals. Many coaches set targets for the team that they have come up with themselves without any input from others. If goals are set by the collective in a more *bottom-up* approach, it develops a sense of accountability and motivation to reach the goal. This doesn't mean that leaders have no say in the process of developing goals, but rather they should play a more facilitative role and guide the group whenever it gets stuck.

Leaders may also recognize that the group is not challenging themselves enough when the leaders see greater potential possible. Having a more democratic approach to goal setting tends to be more effective in the long term.

As shown previously in setting individual objectives, the 100-day plan can also be an effective method for team goal setting. Setting clear and shared goals is one of the conditions for group flow: they bring everyone's attention to a unified vision and target. If you had shown up in Houston at NASA in the 1960s and asked everybody—the janitor, the engineer, the astronauts—what they were trying to do, they all said, "We're putting a man on the moon." There was a clear vision, and everyone knew what their goal was and how to get there.

If you are using the 100-day plan as a framework, start with what you want to accomplish by the end of the year and break it down piece by piece, block by block until you have some workable and actionable steps to take towards the bigger outcome. Weekly or monthly check-ins are valuable here as well so that you can introduce feedback systems to make sure the team is on track.

Performance profiling can be another useful feedback tool to measure and track progress. Both individuals and teams can use this; individual members can rate themselves on various targets they set, or that are set by the coach or trainer. The trainer and the athlete can then use these targets in the evaluation process periodically. Or the group itself can come up with several targets that they feel are important, and as a group rate each skill or attribute from 1-10.

Team Exercise: Create a team goal-setting plan

Using the 100-Day Plan as your goal-setting framework, sit down as a team, and develop some objectives that are in line with the team's values. What do you want to accomplish as a team in the next 365 days? What are some macro and micro goals associated with this outcome goal?

Tip: Keep your values in mind when setting goals. If you have a value to "always compete", then maybe setting a high goal of finishing top three would be appropriate. Or, if the value is more about positive youth development, then results shouldn t be a priority.

* * *

GROUP MINDFULNESS

Great teams have a culture of focus. This doesn't necessarily mean the group practices daily meditations (though I highly recommend this!), but that there are systems in place that remind individuals of the process of staying focused. This could, for example, come in the form of ways to 'check-in' and 'check-out' before and after the work is done. Depending on the team culture, this can be done as a group, such as a team huddle before/after practice, or allowing people to have the space to develop their own routines of bringing their attention to the task and then letting go of the day once the work is done.

This is a simple way to get people to mindfully bring their attention to where they are and develop complete concentration and a sense of control, which in turn creates the opportunity for the other social triggers of group flow mentioned before, such as close listening, good communication, and blended egos. Only when you have practiced paying attention are you able to listen to others without judgment.

The external environment can also be set up for mindfulness. Having designated areas for specific purposes such as a locker room, or meeting space allows for pattern recognition; it reminds our minds that this space is for something specific. Furthermore, as cliche as it sounds, posting certain phrases, quotes, or pictures around the locker room or clubhouse that represent the team's identity and values can act as a reminder of the team's goals and tasks. A famous example is the *This is Anfield* sign over the entrance to the field at Liverpool F.C.'s Anfield Stadium. The home team touches the sign overhead every time they walk out onto the pitch which provides the athletes a sense of pride and identity, reminding them what it means to play there.

It's important that team members have a say in developing their environment and that it is not forced upon them. Only when the team has developed ownership of their values and shared objectives can they start setting up environmental cues to bring their attention to said values and objectives. Values and norms change over time and so it is critical to re-evaluate from time to time and introduce some novelty in order not to become stagnant.

Team Exercise: Mindful Moments

What are some ways for your team to "check-in", both with themselves and as a group? Is your external environment set up to remind athletes to pay attention and focus on the mission? Have a team meeting to discuss how the team values and philosophy can be embodied externally, and how each member will contribute to making sure focus on the process is kept.

Tip: By having teammates share what works individually for each of them, while partaking in close listening, equal participation, and good communication, ideas will come together for ways to foster space for mindful moments.

* * *

GO FAST, OR GO FAR

Getting a group of individuals to work together in pursuit of a common objective is extremely difficult. There are so many different variables that affect team cohesion and it is as much of an art as it is a science. Great leaders don't ask the question, "How do I motivate others?" but rather, "How can I foster an environment where people will motivate themselves?"

Providing a clear objective, feedback, and the autonomy to make choices goes a long way in ensuring the environment is likely to produce flow experiences, and as a result, bring the success we all want. When leaders foster an environment that satisfies the needs of personal autonomy, a sense of belonging, and increased feelings of competence, individual members will be more motivated and inclined to help each other out and go above and beyond for their team. You are more likely to work harder for something you believe in.

Environments that force people to compete against one another create a fear of making mistakes which leads to dysfunctional performance. But when we create a sense of competing *with* one another, the group is running towards an objective rather than away from something. Not being afraid of making mistakes allows space for people to compete to be better. This is because when we feel stress, our bodies release cortisol which impairs rational thinking and decision making. Thus, in a toxic culture, we are biologically more likely to make a bad decision or do something that is ethically questionable. Wouldn't it make sense then, to foster a place where we have the psychological safety to expand our potential without the fear of judgment or exclusion?

Applying the three components of Mental Performance Training is not a quick fix that solves a team's problems. It takes a lot of work from each member of the organization to make things happen. But with patience, constant reflection, and an intrinsic sense of enjoyment we can tackle the most complicated challenges as a team. An old African proverb puts it best:

"If you want to go fast, go alone. If you want to go far, go together."

In Part 2 of this book, I introduced the Mental Performance Training (MPT) framework for individual and team flow. Training the body without the mind will only get you so far, so make sure you are spending equal amounts of time doing both. Next, in Part 3, I will teach you how to adequately recover from the stressors of high performance.

RECAP

- Flow is not only an individual phenomenon, as social beings, we also experience *group flow.*

- The conditions of group flow are built upon many of the individual triggers of flow but require social elements to amplify its effects.

· Teams that experience group flow are more likely to perform better.

· Group cohesion is the tendency for a group to work together in pursuit of a common objective. It can come in the form of task cohesion (how the group tends to focus on a goal and performance); and social cohesion (the degree to which the group enjoys each other's company outside of the performance context, such as going out together and forming friendships).

· Mental Performance Training can be done on a team level as well, developing the core skills of self-awareness, clear objectives, and mindfulness.

III

PART THREE: RECOVERING FROM FLOW

*"The only Zen you find on tops of mountains is the Zen you
bring up there."*
–Robert M. Pirsig

8

THE BURNOUT GENERATION

In Part 1, we discussed the science of flow states and how to achieve a *mind without mind*. Part 2 explored how you can implement Mental Performance Training so that you can make yourself more flow prone and achieve optimal performance. Flow is the most optimal state of consciousness an athlete can achieve, and it can be a powerful performance accelerator. It is particularly helpful in navigating high-stress environments that naturally come with the territory of sport and high performance. Think back to moments in your life that may have been difficult and stressful, but that you now remember as necessary to your growth. A life without challenge is essentially not very exciting, or for that matter, very fulfilling. Humans crave pushing and seeking out our limits. It is just how we are wired.

Csikszentmihalyi talks about how the best moments in our lives are not the passive, receptive, and relaxing times. But rather, the best moments in our lives usually happen when our mind and body are stretched to their limits in a voluntary effort to accomplish something difficult and worthwhile. In other words, flow tends to happen the most when we are actively pursuing something challenging.

However, in order to successfully navigate the challenges that life throws at us we must incorporate times when we take a break from life's ceaseless barrage. There are times when we must step away from the battlefront and recover. Without this period of rest, we potentially risk our health, both mental and physical.

Physical recovery has been a staple of sport science for many years, and we now know that peak performance is not going to happen without recovery. The science on the benefits of sleep, active recovery methods such as icing, stretching, and nutrition are becoming clearer. Taking time to replenish the body is no longer seen as weakness, but rather something required for performance at the highest level.

What is often missing, however, is mental recovery. We don't give our minds enough rest in this new age of constantly being switched on. We have become a generation of burned-out individuals, constantly seeking perfection, pushing on the gas pedal with the fuel on low.

Often, athletes see burnout as something that only occurs physically. We think of overtraining and collapsing from exhaustion after a hard workout. We pride ourselves on experiencing those moments; it means we've trained hard, right? However, this type of behaviour is not sustainable over the long term, and it additionally brings about a less-understood element of burnout: psychological burnout.

For some reason, many of us view the brain as separate from the rest of the body, believing that it somehow requires less fuel and energy. Unfortunately, that is just bad science. It requires the same—if not even more nourishment—as the body in order to function properly. Even slight dehydration will diminish cognitive function, yet we push our minds to the extreme limit and wonder why we suddenly crash. This misunderstanding of the brain's needs can be catastrophic not only to performance but to individual well-being and mental health.

THE DARK SIDE OF FLOW

Seeking ways to get out of our own head can be a dangerous business. In fact, in their book *Stealing Fire,* Jamie Wheal and Steven Kotler did some math on the *altered states economy;* the many ways we seek to get out of our own head whether that is through drugs, personal growth (self-help books), media (social media, movies, pornography, etc.), and recreation (action sports, gambling). They calculated that Americans spend around $4 trillion dollars a year on altering their states of consciousness[91]. Seems like we humans will do anything to not think for a while!

Of course, this comes with its downfalls. Athletes who achieve peak experiences from BASE jumping, for example, search for greater and greater heights and more difficult jumps in order to achieve the optimal balance between challenge and skill. This increase shifts their risk baseline and they require a greater amount of risk to get the same feeling they had the first time they jumped. These individuals have built up a tolerance and require more stimulation. Needless to say, this comes with a certain amount of complications.

In his doctoral dissertation at John F. Kennedy University, Dr. Brent Hogarth, sport psychologist, performance coach for the Flow Research Collective, and a friend of mine explored the fact that high-risk sports (such as Big Wave Surfing or other "extreme" activities) involve high rates of exercise addiction, injury, and death. The perceived sense of control and other enjoyable qualities in flow can be deeply rewarding but can also lead to a dependency and even addiction to flow. This can also create difficulties coping with mundane daily life where flow is absent. Indeed, athletes seeking high-flow states may be at increased risk for emotional dysregulation when they cannot attain flow[92].

It is difficult to not get caught up in chasing the experience of flow, but we must never neglect taking time off to recover. The same lesson applies to everything else we do in life. The more we chase happiness for example, the more it eludes us. Flow can leave us feeling powerful and ready to take on the world, but it shouldn't always be our default state if we want to continue to learn, grow, and evolve.

As such, I thought it would do the experience of flow an injustice if we were to not discuss its darker side. It is of vital importance to understand this concept from more than one side to get a clearer picture of how to handle ourselves and be properly equipped to take back some control when we steer away from our path.

Psychologist Carl Jung did some deep work into the nature of our dark side. He theorized that we all have a "dark side" within us, or as he called it our *shadow* self, and the goal is not to ignore it but rather to understand it in a process he called *individuation.* Everyone has some tendencies they might deem inappropriate or negative, but the more we try to avoid, change, or get rid of these characteristics, the greater power they have over us. The less conflict we have within ourselves, the greater our potential for self-actualization. Luckily, Dr. Hogarth found that mindfulness can be a way to regulate negative emotions and reduce the risk of this "darker" side of flow states.

FILLING THE RIGHT BUCKETS

Bringing mindful awareness to our personality traits can help us navigate high-performance. Traits always have two sides to them, positive and negative. For example, perfectionism has great benefits for athletes. In fact, I would argue that you can't be a high performer without some levels of perfectionism. But that same perfectionism can drive an athlete to burnout, depression, anxiety, and a vast array of other negative consequences. It is a double-edged sword.

Perfectionism stems from a passion and a desire to do better, which is a good thing for athletes. The difference is that the self-aware person knows when to tap into it, and when to let go of unnecessary or unattainable perfection.

That is not to say balance is easy. In fact, I don't believe balance even exists. It really comes down to being self-aware of your priorities and of which areas need to be taken care of at different times.

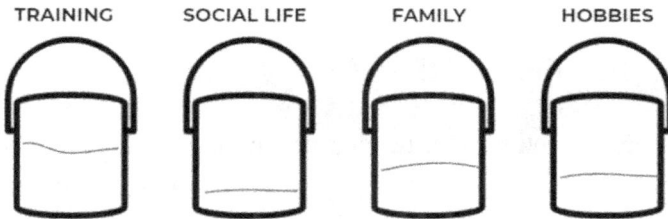

| TRAINING | SOCIAL LIFE | FAMILY | HOBBIES |

Think of the areas in your life more as buckets that need to be filled. You have the family bucket, the career bucket, the personal bucket, and so on. They will never be fully filled all at once since one or more will be less full than the others because we only have a limited amount of water to use. Water in this metaphor relates to the limited physical and mental energy we have. The real skill is learning to decipher which bucket is taking a hit and needs to be refilled and being OK with letting go of another for the time being.

Exercise: Fill up your buckets

Take a piece of paper and list all the areas in your life that are priorities, such as family, training, and socializing. Where do you spend the most time? Are you satisfied with this allocation? What would you change?

* * *

It's OK to spend a lot of time in one area, just be clear on why you are allocating as much energy to that bucket and what the associated costs may be. For instance, if you have decided that spending time with your kids takes priority over training, that's perfectly fine. Just acknowledge this and be aware that your physical goals may take longer to achieve, and plan ahead to maximize each moment you have both for training, and for time with your kids.

FLOW, RECOVER, REPEAT

Now, I am not telling you to give up on your dreams and to stop pursuing mental and physical mastery. What I am trying to get you to understand is that without rest and recovery, peak performance is not possible. Thus, the challenge is to design a life that is filled with optimal experiences with the right checks and balances in place to make sure we don't veer off path into burnout, addiction to flow, and disconnection from other important aspects of our lives.

Ultimately, no one knows what's best for you other than yourself. No amount of self-help books can answer the question of who you really are. But with a greater understanding of peak performance, we can all better optimize our lives (including our pursuit of physical and mental mastery) and diminish the risk of negative consequences.

Flow state is often mistaken for a binary process; either you are in flow or out of flow, on or off. But the reality is that we tend to go through various stages before we experience flow. There is no magic switch, unfortunately, but by being more aware of the different stages of the flow cycle we can begin to understand the mechanisms and roadblocks to consistent high performance.

Herbert Benson, a medical doctor who has contributed more than 190 scientific publications and 12 books, researched the relaxation response in humans and found evidence that we tend to go through various stages in this relaxation response that includes struggle and release[93]. Flow follows a similar four-stage cycle that is constantly in motion. We must thoroughly understand and take care of each stage in order to a) optimize the flow experience, and b) reduce burnout. These four stages are Struggle, Release, Flow, and Recovery.

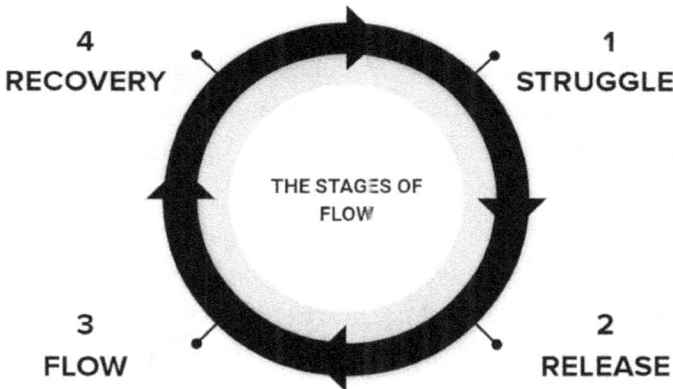

Struggle

When we are involved with a problem or activity, either mentally or physically, we tend to experience struggle. An example of this could be an athlete struggling to find his or her footing in an intense competition. In this stage, our body tends to release *cortisol* and *norepinephrine* signaling the stress response. Most of us tend to want to avoid this stage or are discouraged by its presence; however, we must begin to understand that this is a very necessary stage in the process of achieving flow. Most people actively avoid the struggle, or psych themselves out with negative self-talk and end up not being prepared for the inevitable hardship.

In high-performance situations, suffering is not optional. You can either choose to tap out when things get challenging or embrace the suck and learn to understand and accept the struggle. Applying Mental Performance Training techniques such as breathing, mindfulness, self-talk, and process-oriented goals is crucial to moving on to the next stage.

Release

Once we have accepted the struggle as a crucial ingredient to progression, we are able to release our mental and physical tension and let the process take its course. Physiologically, when our body senses relaxation, it releases nitric oxide. This is a vasodilator, meaning it relaxes the inner muscles of your blood vessels, causing the vessels to widen, increasing blood flow, and lowering blood pressure. The body starts to realize that the mind is not backing down from a challenge and the two start to get in sync. Mentally, we allow space for a mindful response to occur and do not get into a state of paralysis by analysis. An example of this would be a biathlete coming into the shooting portion of the race, taking a moment to breathe deeply to reset, before going through her pre-shot routine. Breathing activates the relaxation response which would benefit the athlete in this anxiety-inducing moment.

Another way to look at release is a detachment from the problem, or rather from our fixation on it. Sometimes stepping away (physically or mentally) can speed up the process of release. Detaching yourself from the problem can help trigger a more pragmatic solution. An athlete can do this by reframing a seemingly bad play as only a temporary occurrence and shifting their attention to the next one. Instead of being fixated on the struggle, the athlete can accept and move on, allowing tension to release.

This even applies to the process of writing this book. Writing can be tedious and grueling with many hours spent struggling over what to write. But I need to trust and let things happen in order to get into a productive (and enjoyable) space for writing, which involves not judging myself for a bad writing session but understanding that on the other side of that struggle is flow. Finding the right blend of discipline and surrender is difficult, but with time and training, you can decipher the right mix for you.

Flow

Flow requires both discipline (struggle), as well as surrender (release). You won't enjoy things as much if you are strict about each little thing you do, nor will completely "letting go" to the flow of life get you closer to the things you seek. A combination of discipline and letting go is a recipe for great things to happen and is likely to bring about the infamous flow state. This is what we trained for!

During this state, selflessness, timelessness, effortlessness, and information richness (STER) are in full force. Dopamine, alongside a few other neurotransmitters, help drive attention to the now. As I've discussed throughout this book, this state is the place where you can achieve great things and also enjoy the moment for what it is.

Recovery

As I've said, once we experience flow, we tend to want to get there more often. However, the Recovery stage is the one stage that is most often neglected in the flow process. Most individuals tend to either ignore or forget the recovery stage thinking more flow is the answer, but too much of a good thing ultimately becomes a bad thing. If we just had an amazing experience such as a great game but don't give ourselves the space to evaluate what happened and learn from it, we are missing out on a whole lot of useful information.

Even at a physiological level, our brain cannot be constantly in flow as we need to bring it back to homeostasis (a relatively stable equilibrium). What comes up, must eventually come down.

Athletes returning home from the Olympics are all too familiar with the concept of the post-Olympics blues. This happens because these athletes worked so hard for four years striving for a medal—sometimes winning and sometimes falling short—and getting caught up in the novelty of the spectacle. And they come back home to the same old boring routine. It can be a challenging transition.

Without recovery we cannot replenish mind, body, or spirit. Planning ahead of time for a rest period after high output and high focus is necessary to refill the tank for the next experience. Things get tricky otherwise and we can run into some negative consequences.

There is a Zen story that encapsulates this idea of recovery perfectly. It goes like this:

> *A number of students were sitting quietly with their teacher one day when a hunter passed by. The hunter was surprised to see the renowned teacher sitting there at ease and doing nothing at all, remarking that the man's inaction appeared to be a waste of precious time.*
>
> *"Take your bow, cock it, and fire an arrow," the teacher responded quietly. And the hunter obliged. "Cock your bow and fire another arrow," the teacher then said.*
>
> *And the hunter again obliged - again and again and again.*
>
> *Finally, the hunter spoke up: "Teacher, if I continue to cock my bow at this rate, it will break.."*
>
> *"The same goes for all of us," said the teacher. "If we push ourselves excessively, we will break too. The right thing to do sometimes is to take a break and cease all activity."*

METHODS OF RECOVERY

There is plenty of scientific evidence that shows taking time off physically and mentally is beneficial for preventing injuries, improving rehabilitation time, improved sleep quality, as well as improved mental health. Athletes need to build micro-moments of recovery into their routines. Let's go over a few ways to incorporate recovery into your life and performance.

Passive Recovery

Passive recovery is the art of doing nothing. This can come in the form of sleeping (which has a tremendous impact on health and performance), or simply resting passively watching TV, or socializing with friends. In the physical sense, it can be greatly beneficial, such as after a heavy workout where the body needs the time to replenish. After all, it is in the rest periods that our muscles grow.

The same goes for passive mental recovery after a long bout of cognitive fatigue. It is important to have passive recovery strategies of literal rest built into your schedule, particularly after prolonged exhaustion. Passive recovery is the most common form of recovery by athletes, but unfortunately often the only form of recovery.

Active Recovery

Most athletes think of recovery as just rest, a complete shut off from the world. Sleep in, binge watch your favourite shows, eating a bunch of food, or having a few drinks. Don't get me wrong, these are all great things to do and we mustn't deprive ourselves of the joys of doing absolutely nothing from time to time, but there is a difference between active and passive recovery. Active recovery is a way to include rest while maintaining momentum.

An example of this could be, for physical recovery, using contrast water therapy (alternating between hot and cold) and stretching, and for mental recovery pursuing other hobbies and interests one might have, such as writing, painting, or playing another sport. The point is not to shut down and do nothing, but rather still to challenge oneself, albeit on a smaller scale, in a completely different environment.

For example, a professional athlete might want to include playing music or writing a book as a way to detach from the daily work of their given sport. This is because anything that we do regularly—even if it starts from a place of passion—eventually turns into a job, and without a way to step away from it for a while, we risk burnout and dissatisfaction.

It almost seems counterintuitive that we would find joy in passive leisure activities; after all, there is so much to keep us pre-occupied nowadays and it is almost considered a sin to be bored. The problem that can come up with passive activities is that we are not being an active participant in leisure anymore, and instead resort to entertaining ourselves passively via stimulation that is externally based, such as social media, watching movies, or browsing the internet, all of which require little to no challenge. Although doing absolutely nothing is sometimes quite necessary, it should not be our default mode of recovery. Engaging only in passive recovery (sleeping, doing nothing, etc.) will not bring us the complete fulfillment we need.

After a hard day at work, try doing some other activity that you've been putting off because you are "too tired" to do it. Often, you will find that this idea that you are "too tired" is just a thought and not a fact. What we crave deep down is to pursue meaningful activities that challenge us and make us better. Even if it is just for an hour or two, the satisfaction and improved well-being you get from these types of activities are more beneficial than the hour or two of passively browsing the internet.

It takes a lot of self-awareness to understand when our mind and body need to rest, and when we just need to step away from being hyper-focused on one particular thing for a while. If you have trouble creating time for recovery in your life, be it passive or active, you may consider scheduling recovery.

One of the athletes I've worked with had this exact problem. They were very meticulous down to the finest detail of when and where they will work out, but they reported feeling overtrained and on the verge of burning out. The very idea of recovery was preposterous, they thought: after all, the more work I put into this, the more I will get out of it, right?

As we worked together though, they realized that their mind and body were screaming for rest. But they did not know where to begin. So, we started with incorporating rest and recovery into their already structured training schedule.

If we plan ahead for something, we are more likely to follow through on it. If you are having difficulty in this area, start with even just one day of recovery. More importantly, give yourself permission to passively recover. We often feel guilty about not being productive every second of every day and this is just an unfortunate by-product of our "always switched on" mentality. It is up to us to take back the reins and regain control of our lives. No one will take time off for you.

Tip: It is all about the challenge/skills balance; if you are feeling too challenged, include more passive recovery days. If you are too bored on the other hand, include more active recovery. Use the goal-setting technique described in Part 2 to get yourself started, and make sure to measure and track recovery just like you would any technical or physical skill.

Play as Recovery

One form of active recovery that we as adults have somehow forgotten and discarded as being useless, is play. Not only have we stopped doing things for fun ourselves, we force children to take things seriously as we the adults do, as if we have it all figured out. Young athletes nowadays spend the majority of the year totally immersed in one sport. They are taken out of physical education classes at school because their club coach wants them to train or prepare for a tournament. They spend their summers in preparatory camps for the next season. And this is all with kids that are 9-16 years old! We drill these children with individually tailored sport programs, and two-a-day training sessions which are then used to weed out the great from the average. Why are we so caught up with creating the next Under-9 world champion? What happened to play?

In what has become an increasing trend over the years, an influx of physically illiterate athletes have come up the ranks. Top-level pros come to their physiotherapists and strength and conditioning coaches with chronic injuries and burnout symptoms because of one fundamental reason: they did not take the time to play and learn different fundamental movement patterns. David Epstein, author of *The Sports Gene: Inside the Science of Extraordinary Athletic Performance*, states:

> "The number one predictor of adult-style overuse injury in a kid
> is that they were highly specialized. So, they had given up, I think
> by age 12, all of their sports to focus only on one, and they were
> doing that sport at least ... nine months a year."[94]

Over-specialization, in short, is becoming an epidemic in sport. Children are not learning the motor (and cognitive) skills that are taught through un-adulterated play. Not only is this having negative effects on their susceptibility to injury, but also on their creativity, and passion for sports and physical activity.

During recess in elementary school, I remember developing and creating new types of games with my friends. For example, we combined elements of soccer, hockey, and tennis, and created *sockey*, where we kicked around a tennis ball into a small net guarded by a goalie wearing hockey pads and gloves. We looked forward to gym class, playing the different types of sports that taught us to jump, roll, catch, kick, fall, and most importantly, fail. This is what physical literacy is all about: learning how your body moves. Without this fundamental skill, our minds and bodies are not in sync.

Many of the greatest athletes of all time, such as Wayne Gretzky and Michael Jordan, played multiple sports growing up. They were great athletes who knew how to manipulate their bodies in space. Steve Nash, who got his first basketball at age 13, credits his soccer background for making him a great basketball player. All the skills these athletes learned from playing different sports helped them to become great at the one they eventually chose to spend the most time on.

What exercise genetics shows us is that trainability is the most important kind of talent, and that it might be completely uncorrelated to how good your baseline is at certain athletic skills. Pete Carroll, former USC, and now Seattle Seahawks Football coach says,

> "The first questions I'll ask about a kid are, 'What other sports does he play? What does he do? What are his positions? Is he a big hitter in baseball? Is he a pitcher? Does he play hoops?'"[95]

What we need is to create an environment that is ripe for development which, includes incorporating more play as not only a means for improved performance, but as a form of recovery. The pressure we put on young, up-and-coming prodigies messes with their emotional and psychological well-being. Wouldn't we rather have happy, creative, and passionate athletes who play the game because they love to, instead of high strung, on-edge individuals who end up burned out or injured because they spend all their time focusing on just one type of performance goal?

If a child loves the game, those who have the choice to train while also doing other activities they enjoy will find a way to be better at that sport more diligently than those who are forced to robotic-ally train, day in and day out, with no time to be a kid. And even as adults: better coaches and training will undoubtedly help us get better, but the impact of free, unstructured, flow-inducing play can help us hone our talents, learn about our bodies, and enjoy life, which will make our performance that much greater in the long run.

We must develop an environment where children are free to try differ-ent things. The skills they learn—on the street or in the backyard—will stay with them for life. Let go of the reins a bit and allow them to process things on their own. They don't need to be the best 12-year-old athlete in the country.

Time off can give you the space to develop a sense of curiosity and wonder again for your craft. Here, we cultivate the beginner's mind. With a beginner's mind, you are no longer bound by what you think you know about a given activity, but instead are able to see it with fresh eyes, much like that of a child who examines things for the first time.

Create a Self-Determined Environment

It is not just the individual that must make these changes in their routine, but the environment itself needs to be conducive to play and enjoyment. Individuals, especially children, grow in an environment that promotes the natural process of learning and growth, just like a seed grows into a tree only if the environment nourishes it.

Using the three basic needs proposed by Self-Determination Theory (autonomy, relatedness, competence), we can manipulate the environ-ment to allow space for optimal motivation and long-term participation. For example, stronger adherence to exercise programs was found with instructors who fostered an autonomy-supportive environment where they cultivated the use of positive language and gave reasons behind the exercises they assigned[96]. Exercisers were free to make their own choices through positive reinforcement, which created more space to understand why they exercise, and ultimately led to long term motivation.

Our environment shapes our experience and thus creates a supportive climate where people feel autonomous, interact socially, and experience mastery of a task, which will determine how much enjoyment they have. Once an individual feels like they have the confidence to take on an activity, they can build the intention to create a prolonged behaviour pattern.

On the contrary, if the individual has negative experiences in their training environment, such as forced over-specialization, they may develop lower perceptions of their own attitude, self-image, and competence. This stops them from forming meaningful habits that will help them achieve success. Therefore, if programs and activities prioritize enjoyment, they will create happy, healthy athletes and teams who are motivated to continue reaching for their goals with their given activity.

RECAP

· Flow isn't a binary process. It follows four stages:

1. Struggle
2. Release
3. Flow
4. Recover

- Recovery is often neglected or misunderstood but is essential for flow. Recovery can be passive such as sleeping or watching a show, or it can be active such as icing and stretching or pursuing a hobby.

- Make sure you incorporate playfulness as a form of recovery. Taking things too seriously all the time is a recipe for burnout.

- Environments that promote the three basic human needs - Autonomy, Competence, and Relatedness - are more likely to increase motivation and well-being. This is the premise behind self-determination theory.

9

PROTECT YOUR ATTENTION

We are increasingly connected to everyone around us. A family member across the ocean is just a video call away. But all this connection has come with a cost. We are pummeled with information and connection that it becomes too much for our primitive minds to handle. To put it into perspective, we now have access to more knowledge in our pockets than a monk during the middle ages would acquire in his lifetime. Such a vast increase in the availability of knowledge makes it more difficult to discern what information is true and as such we may find it increasingly hard to understand what is important to us. Economist Herbert A. Simon puts it best:

"A wealth of information creates a poverty of attention."[97]

High-performance sport can be a daunting task in today's world. Whether you are a promising young athlete deciding where to go to school, professional navigating negative criticism on social media, or a weekend warrior trying to find the motivation to exercise, we all suffer from an overload of input on a daily basis. This is because the brain can only take so much. Put simply, after too many mental calculations, we get tired. This is known as decision fatigue. Even though we can search for any piece of information we want in a few seconds, we cannot possibly search, process, and learn all the information available to us; our brains are simply limited in their capacity for intake. When we have too much information to process, we often get stuck trying to make decisions. This "paralysis by analysis" trap is eloquently illustrated in the poem, Centipede Dilemma:

A centipede was happy - quite!

Until a toad in fun

Said, "Pray, which leg moves after which?"

This raised her doubts to such a pitch,

She fell exhausted in the ditch,

Not knowing how to run.

REDUCE THE NOISE

Now more than ever the strongest skill we can possess is the ability to eliminate distractions and simplify our focus. I like to call this process *reducing the noise.* Focus itself is not so much the act of focusing on a task as much as it is eliminating the things pulling at your attention. Whether that is the dopamine rush of checking your notifications or the difficult conversation you had with a friend, reducing the noise means deciphering what in your life is causing you to be pulled away from the present moment, and learning not to act upon that craving. The goal is to not *crave* attention but to *pay* attention.

During a game, it's not going to help an athlete to focus on the crowd, a mistake, or on the scoreboard, as these are unrelated to the task at hand, which is to focus on the play. A student studying for an exam loses focus when they have ten tabs open at the same time (two of which are social media). In both cases, the individuals would be better served by creating environmental conditions to support their own success, and which keep their objectives simple and clear. As Bruce Lee once said,

"It's not the daily increase but daily decrease. Hack away at the unessential. Simplicity is the key to brilliance."

Focus is one of the primary flow triggers. This means that to be more likely to experience flow and *no mind* reduce all the attention-grabbing variables in your life and focus on one thing at a time. Quality over quantity.

Take a moment to reflect on something you want to accomplish. How often do you get distracted when you work towards that goal? What pulls at your attention? When you're on the field, or performing your chosen activity, where is your mind? It seems like a silly question, but too often we don't realize our mind is not where it should be. Too many things take us away from what we're trying to do in that moment. We are stuck with being physically present, but mentally absent. This leads to decreased performance and ultimately lowers happiness and well-being.

Reducing the noise doesn't have to be complicated. It starts with small incremental choices and eventually you find yourself taking back control of your life. Here are a few things you can start doing to begin the process.

- Get a piece of paper and pen and make a list of attention grabbers or distractions in your life and performance. Reflect on which ones you have the ability to control and then how you can reduce their impact. For example, this may mean putting your phone away when studying or moving away from a distracting teammate during a drill. As a reminder, post your plans for remaining focused somewhere you are likely to see them.

· Create a most important task list (MIT). Write down the 3-5 most important tasks you want to get done today or this week. It doesn't matter if you complete them or not, at least you set the intention to focus. This will give you a clear objective, which is another condition for flow.

· Practice mindfulness. As we discussed in previous chapters, with mindfulness—the practice of non-judgmental present moment awareness—we are training our minds to focus on the task at hand. Spending even just a few minutes each day following the breath and bringing your attention back to it when you get distracted can affect all of your life and performance skills. For example, you will be better able to notice yourself drifting off during practice when the coach is talking and bring that attention back to the moment. And in your non-athletic life, you can bring yourself back to the moment if you find yourself drifting off during a conversation with a loved one. Remember, flow follows focus.

· If you are a student alongside training for your sport, set your work/study periods into smaller chunks. Our brains don't like big goals. We can only sustain our attention for a limited time. What has been shown to be effective is working in bursts of small chunks of time (around 25 minutes), with 5-minute breaks in between. The Pomodoro technique uses this format. I use it all the time in writing blogs, creating presentations for workshops, and in fact, I am using it right now as I write this. I find it highly effective.

It's tough to feel like you're getting anything done when there are a million things competing for your attention. Focus is becoming an extremely prized commodity in modern-day society. Start improving your focus by spending a few minutes out of your day distraction-free and see where that leads.

SOCIAL MEDIA AND FOCUS

Over the last few decades, the digital age has brought about some beneficial changes for humans, such as providing a voice for the otherwise unheard and bringing light to societal issues and change. However, social media use has also come with a cost. With all this digital connection we are constantly on display and always online. Comparison, jealousy, and loneliness are just a few of the symptoms of constant social media use, and we are beginning to see a steady decline in mental health, especially with youth.

Many scientists, and even the social media engineers themselves, directly correlate the rise of social media to this decline in mental health. We can see a steep jump in the rates of depression, anxiety, and suicide since social media burst into the scene in 2008. There is competition for our attention and if we do not form a healthy relationship with social media, we risk it affecting not only our performance, but our well-being.

We've all been there, mindlessly scrolling through our feeds looking at the highlights of other peoples' curated lives, which leaves us feeling worse and worse with each scroll. Thirty minutes later, we feel inferior and begin to doubt our own journey.

We must understand that this is not our fault. These platforms are designed to compete for our attention and keep us scrolling for as long as possible. Our brains are very susceptible to novelty (a flow trigger, after all) and, combined with our primal need for social connection, we can fall down a pretty deep social media rabbit hole.

Social media has also started to affect how we view exercise and has altered our motivations for it. For example, after tracking a recent run with an app, I received a thumbs up from someone else for my achievement (I beat a personal best). As I walked home basking in my sense of accomplishment, I had the urge to share this with the world. I rarely use external apps to monitor my runs, using them sparingly to get some feedback on my progress so when I received a notification that someone liked my update, I suddenly had the urge to let more people know.

But then I caught myself and tried to see this urge a bit more objectively, as one does when practicing mindfulness. What would be the reason to post this accomplishment? If no one knows about it, does the personal best mean nothing?

It's an interesting dilemma. Some studies show that sharing your exercise with others on social media can improve motivation to exercise since you feel a sense of relatedness and connection to others[98]. But there is also a dark side to this sharing. The authors of the study report:

> "When interactions are not positive – actions such a negative comment about your own exercise behaviour or attempt, or even negative social comparison with others exercise endeavors – it

can lead to feeling disconnected from others, which, in turn, negatively affects exercise motivation."

And that's not the only thing that is negative about sharing your achievements. When individuals set a goal that is closely tied to their identity and then share their intentions with other people, they are actually less likely to achieve the goal. This was demonstrated in a study where researchers looked at whether or not scientists are more likely to write their papers if they tell their colleagues about their intentions. Lo and behold, the more the scientists talked about the action, the less likely they were to actually do it[99]. This is because we get a similar dopamine hit from saying we are going to do something as when we actually do it. It's a cheaper way to get our fix!

On the one hand, social media can help motivate some people to get started with exercise, but on the other, it can cause an obsession with sharing only your best self. It is tough to find the right balance between the two, but at the end of the day, we must understand that if we are too reliant on judgments and other factors outside of ourselves (known as external motivation), our motivation tends to be short-lived and we are less in control of our progress. People who have goals that are internally motivated, or in other words behaviours they do just for sheer enjoyment, are more likely to stick with those behaviours for the long run.

Not everyone is going to like us, or for that matter care that we just ran a 5 km PB, so by seeking external approval we are barking up the wrong tree.

All is not doom and gloom, however, if we learn to become aware of our triggers and the habits that may not be conducive to our overall mental health. Social media can be a useful tool and it is unrealistic to think we all should completely go off the grid (unless you're one of the few that have—kudos to you!). Instead, we can form a healthier relationship with these tools and live a more balanced life, on our own terms.

Exercise: <u>Reflect on your social media use</u>

Answer honestly: how is your relationship with social media? How much time do you spend on these platforms? Are they providing you with value, or do they detract from your goals and aspirations?

* * *

Another thing to question is what triggers your need to check your phone. Pay attention to the subtle details of your habits such as always going for your phone whenever you feel sad, which is something psychologists call experiential avoidance: the attempts to avoid thoughts, feelings, memories, physical sensations, and other internal experiences—even when doing so creates harm in the long-run.

The next time you start to reach for your phone, stop and ask yourself, "Why am I going for my phone"? Is this just a habit? Am I bored? Lonely? The more we question the "why" behind our habits the more we can understand and develop better ones.

Take up journaling and reflect on your experiences with social media and soon you will notice the patterns. You will start to notice how you feel after you go through your feed. Do you feel satisfied or happy? Or do you feel restless, envious, or bad about yourself? Some feel that there is an illusion of sustenance in this age of instant gratification, while others feel connected and engaged on social media. In any case, the more we are aware of our habits and any self-perpetuating cycles in which we are engaged, the more we can build habits that increase our well-being. Keeping track of how you feel and the things that affect it can drastically improve your outlook.

Here are some more tips for evaluating your relationship with the internet and/or your phone:

Social Media Sabbath

Since social media can become a hindrance to our pursuit of flow, we need a way to check how much of a distraction it really is. A "social media sabbath" is a good way to do this. Every week, I have one full day free from social media use. Sometimes I even plan a week off social media, especially when I start to notice my mental health is being affected by seeing all the curated "highlight reels" posted to my social media feeds. These often give me a sense of unrealistic standards that I shouldn't feel the need to live up to. I even did a thirty-day challenge, which taught me a lot including the fact that no, the world did not end when I wasn't on social media. Everything goes on business as usual and you really don't miss out on much.

Try it out yourself. You don't have to start with thirty days. Start with one day out of the week to completely go cold turkey from social media. If you find it difficult to last one day, reflect on that and consider what that means for your life. Is that how you truly want to spend your time? Think back to the goals you set earlier in this book. Do they align with your social media use?

Don't be too hard on yourself though, remember that these platforms are designed to hack your attention and it takes some time to form better habits. We are all guilty of checking our phones too often, but with some time and training, we can form better, healthier relationships with them and protect our precious attention. Be patient and start off with smaller more realistic goals such as going offline for an hour to start.

Limit Your Use

Most phones have a built-in well-being function to limit app usage. For example, I have a 15-minute timer on social media, and cannot open it after 9:00 PM. I also blocked one full day a week as my "social media sabbath." I have found myself to be more productive and I spend less time needlessly and mindlessly scrolling. What's more, seeing your monthly usage data can be quite eye-opening (and scary)!

Out of Sight, Out of Mind

One time-tested psychological trick is to physically remove the thing trying to hold your attention. I keep my phone charging in another room when I sleep, and I try to keep it out of arm's reach when doing work or even watching TV. For those of you who like to use your phone as an alarm, you can drop that excuse. There are many alarms you can buy for cheap that can replace your phone.

Mindful Consumption

Plan ahead and create the space for more mindful phone use. Next time you are out with your friends or family, see if you can just have your phone in your pocket instead of on the table. Practice tuning into the present (and what you are potentially avoiding by using your phone) rather than drifting away to a digital world.

At the end of the day, it is you who must decide whether or not your relationship with your phone and social media is hindering or helping your performance and well-being. It starts with being honest with yourself. Understand that many of us struggle with similar distractions. However, it is becoming more and more clear that the individuals who can hold their attention the longest, without getting distracted by a thought, feeling (or a ding of a phone!) hold great power in this age of attention poverty. Time to reduce the noise, my friends!

GRATITUDE & PERSPECTIVE

With more of our identity on display online and the constant comparison with others, it is easy to forget how good we actually have it. If you have a roof over your head and, somewhere to sleep and eat, then you are better off than a big majority of the world's population. With so much excess nowadays, we need to remind ourselves of our good fortune on a consistent basis. Viewed from a sufficient distance, all our problems seem pretty insignificant.

For example, is the fact that you missed an empty net during your last game really that big of a deal? Did anyone get hurt? Are you still breathing? In most cases, nothing has really changed, and guess what? Most people don't even care. The sooner you can shift your perspective to the bigger picture, the easier it is to let go of minor inconveniences. This then allows us to be grateful for what we have and create space for more flow experiences.

We need to practice searching for the good in any situation because the more we can force our minds to look for the positives on a consistent basis, the more we can have that as our default mindset. Despair tends to be cheap and easy to come by and optimism can sometimes be difficult. But training for a positive and grateful mindset will increase motivation, which increases focus. This in turn creates a mind free to pay attention to the task at hand—a *mind without mind.*

We explore optimism by practicing gratitude. Being grateful helps put our daily lives into perspective and allows for mental recovery from stress. For example, if you've had a game (or an entire day) that you perceived as bad; ask yourself: what three things went relatively well? There is always something we can find if we dig deep enough.

Exercise: Gratitude training

At the start of each day, try and pick three things you are grateful for to get the day off on the right foot. Then, at the conclusion of each day reflect on three wins or amazing things that happened.

Examples include getting a good night's sleep, sunny weather, being healthy, a great conversation with a friend, getting a workout in despite not feeling like it, and completing a project.

* * *

Through shifting our perspective on our life and performance, we can allow the space for gratitude to emerge and in turn train our minds for optimism. We have evolved as pessimists, scanning the external environment for threats to our survival which has done us well for most of human history. But most things these days aren't life-threatening, so we must understand that this ingrained pessimism is just how our brains are wired. But by applying a little awareness and training our brains to focus on the good, we can re-learn optimism, and begin to believe that despite all the negative things that are happening, something good is just around the corner.

Optimism and gratitude aren't about ignoring the bad in life, but rather about seeing these difficulties through a wider lens. To always be happy is an unrealistic goal, and one that quite frankly wouldn't even be that enjoyable because it is going through the darkness that makes you appreciate the light. Life works in this balancing way, and you cannot have the good without the bad.

I like to use surfing as a wonderful metaphorical lesson for life. You're not always going to find the perfect wave. Some waves are great, some are not. If we were able to catch every single wave, then surfing wouldn't be as fun because the challenge would significantly decrease. Patience is an important skill: sometimes we're riding the wave in flow, sometimes we're getting pummelled by the water. We can't control the waves, but we can most definitely learn to surf.

RECAP

- Your attention is a precious commodity. You need to protect it at all costs. Make a list of things that create a lot of "noise" for you and do your best to reduce their impact.

- Despite its potential for connecting people, recent research about social media is highlighting potential negative consequences such as increased depression and anxiety caused by the constant comparison with peers. Taking time off social media can have great benefits for increasing attention and reducing the noise.

- Gratitude training is a great way to train your brain to focus on optimism and to see things from a different perspective. There are many apps and journals you can use such as the *5 Minute Journal* that prompt you with gratitude exercises.

10

LIVE SLOW, FIND FLOW

We can learn a lot by just noticing nature. Nature does not rush things or force things to happen, yet everything is accomplished. There is a certain harmony in this effortless effort. In this age of constant pursuit and self-improvement, we may benefit from a little more passiveness. However, this is not to be confused with laziness. We would never consider water or trees to be lazy, would we? Trees can often withstand hundreds of years of drought, storms, and winters and remain rooted in the ground.

But for some reason, we tend to idolize the "go-getters" and "busy-bees" who seem to have a ceaseless drive for improving themselves. There is nothing wrong with wanting to improve, but it does sometimes come with a cost. How much self-improvement is too much? Where is the limit to the constant pursuit of betterment?

There is a difference between self-actualization and *self-image* actualization. Bruce Lee talked about how most of us don't really know ourselves. Often, we spend time trying to enhance our image of ourselves rather than doing the deep work of really getting to the core of who we are[100]. In our current day of constant comparison, self-analysis, and tracking and measuring, many of us may have lost sight of what we are actually striving for. It seems we might be self-improving ourselves to death.

Now I am not here to tell you to throw in the towel. After all, I am in the business of improving performance. What I would like to argue is that we have become so fixated on the idea of improving everything about ourselves that we never stop to question what it's all really for.

We are all guilty of putting too much on our plate. Often, we want to juggle a healthy lifestyle of eating right, exercising at least three times a week, pursuing a meaningful career, learning a new skill, and on top of it all, finding a suitable partner. Eventually, something is going to give. Anxiety disorders are steadily rising, which as some studies show, are correlated with the rise in perfectionism in millennials[101].

Take things such as running apps for example: they have improved accountability and performance for both weekend warriors and elite athletes, but without careful use, these performance statistics can become a heavy burden of constant striving and obsession. We may see ourselves no longer satisfied with breaking a personal record as our mind drifts towards the next record to hit, in a constant cycle of one-upping ourselves. We may win a gold medal or hit a personal best without spending a moment to appreciate it.

Striving for perfection is a noble pursuit, but left unchecked it becomes a lifestyle full of unrealistic checklists. We are not capable of beating a personal best every week or winning every championship. What we should be striving for rather than perfection or mastery, is mastering the pursuit of mastery itself.

PLAY THE LONG GAME

A common theme these days is the need to be perfect. Previous generations grew up comparing themselves to the Joneses' down the street, but nowadays the Joneses' include everyone on the internet. We often compare our behind-the-scenes realities with everyone else's highlight reels and we can't help but think, "am I enough?" or "am I *doing* enough?"

Don't get me wrong: having high standards is synonymous with high performance. You need to set your sights high and far in order to get to the greatest levels of performance, if you desire that. This high achievement does, however, sometimes come with a cost. When we start to paint each moment in time as black or white, win or lose, do or die, we start to walk down a dangerous path. The truth is that it will never be enough. There is always something more we can do to be better. But the reason for striving to be better often gets lost in translation along the way.

There is no use in being the best when being the best comes at the expense of your happiness and well-being. This is the secret that experienced athletes and performers understand sometimes too late. Their whole lives, they have strived towards making a name for themselves and reaping all the external rewards they can dream of. Somewhere along the line they forget the reason why they started in the first place.

We have been taught from a young age that if we *do* more, we will find the success we want. All we need to do is to put in more hours at the gym or training ground and good things will come. Although putting in effort is definitely part of the equation for success, it is not the entire formula. We need to emphasize the being and not just the doing. If we are able to *be* more present—more authentic, more compassionate to ourselves—the doing will come naturally as a result.

However, if we identify ourselves solely with the doing, everything becomes one dimensional in the form of success or failure; our self-worth and our drive to achieve become fragile. Our definition of success shouldn't depend on whether or not we win that gold medal. What starts off as a desire to be better can lead to an unhealthy obsession that, in theory, won't stop until we achieve what we see as perfection; but often, our false views of success get in the way, and we never reach that perfect place. Any pursuit, however worthy and desirable, becomes a disease when the mind is obsessed with it.

Many athletes have become obsessed with greatness without ever defining what it means. Who is the greatest athlete of all time? Can we ever objectively answer that question? Was it the person who won the most trophies and scored the most points? Or maybe it was the one who had a career filled with mostly mediocrity, yet managed to gracefully transition to other ventures and stay happy and healthy with plenty of friendships and stories to share?

I am not here to tell you which one is the right path for you; you need to decipher that for yourself. There is nothing wrong with pursuing excellence as long as you define what that means to you. But understand this: perfection or mastery can never really be attained; they can only be strived for. Instead of the pursuit of mastery, we need to get better at mastering the pursuit. What are you pursuing, and how do you measure success? Do you have the long game in mind? Here are a few insights that might help guide you in this process.

Work is infinite, time is finite. You can always do more work. There is no limit to the things you can do. But if we are mindlessly doing more just to do more we are walking into a trap. There will always be more work to do, but we are limited in the time given to us. Let's make sure we are making the most of our time by doing the things that actually make us happy.

Define what success means to you. What are you really striving towards? What is the end goal? These are questions we seldom ask ourselves. Most of us want to be happy, but there are many avenues to take towards that goal. Maybe you want to relentlessly pursue greatness and become the Greatest of All Time (G.O.A.T). That is an amazing dream and I hope the techniques in this book inspire you to reach that goal. But make sure you understand that, if this is your goal, other areas in your life will take a hit. Success isn't about how your life looks to others: it's about how it feels to you. Make sure you pursue things that truly matter to you and forget the rest.

Balance doesn't really exist. It is very difficult to balance a high-performance career, with children, a spouse, and other pursuits and passions. Some of your buckets will be fuller than the others. Don't try to keep each bucket perfectly even, but rather sit down and consider which bucket needs to be filled to a certain level in order for you to stay focused on your priorities. And remember that different buckets will be more important than others at different times in your life. At one stage of your life, the sport bucket may be full. During another stage, playing ball with your children may be more fulfilling to you than work. Ask yourself what really matters in my life now? Keep your priorities simple and real, and remember that you get to choose what your priorities are at any given time.

Don't judge yourself. There is no manual for life or performance. We are all trying to figure it out. The only way to get the experience, is to have the experience.

Embrace the suck. Apply more mindfulness to your performance and learn to see failure as a necessary ingredient to success. Things are going to be tough out there, and there will be times where it seems unbearable. But the struggle is necessary in order to be ready for flow. Learn to embrace the complex uncertainty that is high performance.

Perfectionism and overidentification with what you do creates little space for mastery and flow. Life isn't meant to be lived one-dimensionally but rather lived to the fullest with as many experiences as possible. As Mihaly Csikszentmihalyi discovered:

> "This paradox of rising expectations suggest that improving the quality of life might be an insurmountable task. In fact, there is no inherent problem in our desire to escalate our goals, as long as we enjoy the struggle along the way. The problem arises when people are so fixated on what they want to achieve that they cease to drive pleasure from the present. When that happens, they forfeit their chance of contentment."

A PERSONAL TALE

I have had the privilege to work with many athletes and to hear their stories. Some have great tales of overcoming challenges; others talk about a big obstacle or failure that they perhaps still struggle with to this day. Whatever the narrative is, it takes a great amount of courage to be able to reflect and share the story of one's life with others. I find it fruitful for myself as a participant in this process to share some of my own stories of doubt, insecurity, success, failure, and everything else that lies on the journey of mastery. In this way, the journey becomes a blending of worldviews and experiences that can diverge and come together to form a clearer path to understanding for all of us involved in the conversation.

In light of this, I feel it might be beneficial to share some highlights of my own path. To perhaps show you that everyone is fighting their own battles, in their own way, in their own time, and if you struggle, you are not alone.

Just because I study the mind does not mean I am immune to negative thinking, anxiety, and a lack of confidence. These are all part of the journey of becoming good at anything. Life doesn't come with a manual. We do something, we fail, we learn, and repeat the process until we succeed.

The mental game is something I always struggled with growing up playing sport. I always knew that technically I was decent enough, but when it came to high-pressure moments, I struggled to deal with the stress of performing. I'd often lack the confidence to perform as well as I knew I could.

There would be times though, where everything fell into place: moments of flow, where I felt unstoppable. My confidence would be through the roof and I would experience *no mind*. I would strive for these peak experiences each and every game. But as it is with chasing flow, the more I tried to attain it, the more it alluded me.

These rare flow states would keep me chasing my dream of playing professional football (soccer) one day, despite my lack of confidence at times. My confidence greatly depended on the environment I was in. I remember having amazingly supportive coaches, who with one word, could make me want to run through walls for them. I was always the type of player who needed a pat on the back and to have someone tell me I was doing OK. Therefore, when I found myself in an environment where the coach was less than supportive (I know some of you know what I am talking about) I would crumble in self-doubt.

A lot of coaches go for a one-size-fits-all method to training, but as it is with most things, every individual learns and perceives things differently. I always wished I could have been the type of player to use criticism as a motivator, but I was definitely not. Criticism hurt my confidence.

However, despite having environments and coaches that hindered my confidence most of the time, I still somehow found enough passion to keep the dream alive. This led me to move abroad after high school to try out for a youth team playing in the first division in Poland. I had a connection with a coach who told me I would be given a shot if I went there. Without giving it much thought, I left family and friends in Canada to pursue this dream.

Things got off to a pretty good start: I made the team after a few weeks, and even scored a goal in my first game. Fast forward a few months though, and it was a different story. Despite speaking the language and having family in Poland, I still felt a bit alienated. I didn't feel accepted by my teammates, and I spent the majority of my time alone as a result. I was also not used to the different coaching style and level of play, which made my performance anxiety worse. This of course led to decreased confidence, and then to poorer and poorer performances. This combined with a number of different factors, brought me to a place that was not good, to say the least.

I was not getting any playing time and was even demoted to playing with the younger reserve team which, as you can imagine can take its toll on the ego of a seventeen-year-old. I did not have the coping skills to deal with being away from home, being rejected by my teammates, and lacking the confidence to perform.

It all came to a thundering conclusion after one particular game, which I very much remember. I was taken off at halftime during a reserve team game for a bad performance, and in front of everyone in the locker room, the coach outright told me that I was having a horrible game and that he was going to replace me with another player.

As the second half was about to start, I remember that everyone left the locker room, and I just sat there devastated. I asked myself: *Am I really that bad? Was this all for nothing?* I was so embarrassed that I took off my gear and left to go home. I decided then and there that the dream had ended; I left without saying goodbye to anyone.

After a rough couple of days going over everything that had gone wrong, I had one of those "now what?" moments. Maybe I was making excuses. Maybe I could have stuck it out a few more months and worked harder. Was I just scared to keep pushing myself in the face of adversity? Did I just desperately want to go home? Or could it have been my coaches, who if they had gotten to know me would have understood that I lacked confidence and needed a bit more support? Would I have thrived under a different style of coaching? Probably. But the reality is that both myself and my coaches could have done better. I could have believed in myself more, and they could have done the same. In sports, as in life, there is no perfect method, just imperfect people trying to make things work the best they can.

I eventually decided that, after a few months of giving it a shot, my dream of a professional football career was over.

Now I had to decide what to do with my life. After some soul searching (mostly Google searching), I came across the field of sport and performance psychology. I figured that perhaps my struggles with the mental game could be of use to other athletes, and thus I set out to make it my mission to help others who were dealing with the same things and to help them cope with these issues in a more effective manner than I had. I came home soon after and began my journey towards learning everything about the psychology of sport and performance.

Though I had to improve my marks in a few classes, I was accepted into University and I made the varsity team my first year. But my mental game was still lacking. The same issues of low confidence and performance anxiety resurfaced; I was not the player I wanted to be. It was a struggle getting playing time that first year.

Heading into the second year of my undergraduate degree, I thought things were looking up. I was actually feeling more confident going into pre-season with the team, thinking that the rookie year was behind me and I would be playing a more prominent role in the team. The coaches had other ideas though: I was cut after the very last pre-season game. This was another devastating blow to an already fragile athlete. I spent that year in denial, not admitting to anyone else that I was not actually on the team. I had such a strong athletic identity, believing that this was who I was. Being cut from the team equated to being a total failure in my eyes.

I have since learned to separate what I do from who I am. Football was just something I did and does not have to define me completely (nor does your sport define you!). I am so much more than that. This was probably one of the greatest lessons I have learned. It has helped me not only become a better athlete, but a happier and more well-rounded individual.

Looking back at all these other "failures" and setbacks, I now understand that they were all learning opportunities. We all have something that holds us back, whether it is physical, mental, or social. There is no use in denying this fact. The more we fight our insecurities, the more control they have over us. The goal of mental training is to become more aware of and to accept these barriers, and to develop the right tools to deal with them. We won't know what those barriers and tools are until we step out of our comfort zone and do the hard-introspective work to learn and grow.

LIVE SLOW, FIND FLOW

I am not trying to argue here that we should stop improving ourselves. What I am trying to say is that we need to get better at questioning why we have the urge to improve any particular aspect of ourselves.

If any goal you have is truly something you are passionate about, go ahead and keep pushing. But having too much on our plate does not create quality outcomes. The way we get better at anything is to fully engage with just one goal at a time. Through mastering the Zen philosophy of no-mind, we can learn to enjoy the moments we have on this Earth with a bit more intention and gratitude. My hope is that you will find more of these moments after reading this book and learn to understand that *you are enough* no matter what you decide to do with the time given to you.

This book is not meant to be a step-by-step guide to make you better. I don't have all the answers for you and your specific issues, because I don't know you personally. But this book does provide a framework for training your mind for peak performance and well-being. Perhaps it will allow you to reach greater success in your performance, or maybe it will give you permission to loosen the reins a bit so that you can recover from your effort. From one athlete to another: I sincerely wish you the best on your journey of mastery.

Do not wish for an easy life, but rather go forth towards the difficult and worthwhile, the tense and nerve-racking moments in your life that make your hair on the back of your neck stand up and make you a little scared.

Because the best moments in our lives are not the passive, receptive, relaxing times, but the moments on the razor's edge of our limits, doubting our abilities but still managing to find the extra ounce of courage to push through. What humans actually need, as Viktor Frankl puts it, "is not a tensionless state but rather the striving and struggling for some goal worthy of them."

MY STORY: WRITING THIS BOOK

Writing this book has been a long and tedious process filled with doubt and insecurity about whether or not my voice will be heard. Am I too vulnerable? Am I not vulnerable enough? Is it scientific enough? Are all the references legitimate and can I trust the research? Is there enough authenticity that my own take on things is clear? These thoughts cross my mind.

I have always been intrigued by the unknown: by the outer edges of psychological understanding. Some of these concepts are not yet clear or may not have the most prestigious journals reporting on them, but I would say that is OK. The whole purpose of scientific inquiry is to explore and question things.

Our knowledge of science and, psychology in particular, is still very limited. I believe acknowledging this fact is the first step towards real scientific investigation of our minds. This internal battle of mind, between using what can be considering as fact, and exploring out-of-the-box concepts was a big factor in the writing process of this book.

When I first started to write, I tried to figure out what I wanted to write about and couldn't get anything down. I struggled with trying to please the psychological sciences, while opening the door for philosophy to re-enter into our everyday vocabulary. I wanted a blend of both worlds but felt pressured to choose.

Eventually, I figured that nothing would ever seem like a good enough idea, so I just decided to simply start off with a few nuggets of research or quotes that spoke to me and go from there. I soon found myself entering a different domain, which was the art of writing. How do you put all that is in your own head onto paper, anyway? As with all forms of creativity, writing is supposed to be spontaneous and from the heart.

I don't know where the book will take me, but it is the unknown that inspires me to write. Of course, there is always the uncertainty of whether or not anyone will ever read the darn thing. But I guess it is in that uncertainty that one finds clarity. Maybe putting pen to paper and writing down what I want to share with you will help me in my own exploration of the inner game.

Life is meant to be lived in the present, and I firmly believe that it shouldn't be seen as something that has a finish line, but rather a journey with many countless beginnings and ends that can only be appreciated by being where you are.

If I worry too much about what I have written, or what I am about to write, then I just get in my own way. In the same way, if you worry too much about your game, your stats, or your performance, these things may suffer. As I've mentioned in this book, mindfulness takes numerous forms, and perhaps applying the non-judgemental and passive approach to observing thoughts can be also applied to writing them down, as well as to playing sports, training, or to any performance in life.

CONCLUSION

In a way, this book is a philosophical manifesto. It all comes down to a simplified purpose: live slow, find flow. For me, living slow doesn't mean being lazy and complacent, but rather slowing things down, recovering from the intensity, and taking in the moment.

Finding flow on the other hand, is about going after the experiences I've mentioned in here: finding moments where the mind is quiet, where we experience *no mind.* This where I find the most joy.

It is the mastery of these two elements: flow and recovery, that I believe set us up for a life of fulfillment without going over the edge into burnout.

I sincerely hope this book provides you with something to build on, so that you can finally get out of your own way and experience a *mind without mind.* In the meantime, follow your feet and be where you are.

RECAP

- The goal of high performance isn't to burn bright and then to quickly fade away. Learn to play the long game of mastery so that you can have a long and meaningful career.

- Pursue things that you enjoy and that you alone have decided on are worthy. Listen to other people but make your own decisions about how you want to spend your life.

- My philosophy ultimately comes down to this: *live slow. find flow.*

Afterword

The various exercises used in this book can be completed with the accompanying workbook available for download at **www.flowperformancepsych.com/workbook-download.** The password to access the file is *NoMind2021.*

Looking to take a deeper dive into flow and mental performance training? Check out Flow Performance at
www.flowperformancepsych.com.

Notes

MIND AND NO MIND

1   Colin O'Brady has had some amazing adventures. This quote was taken from an interview he had on a podcast with Joe Rogan: Rogan, Joe; O'Brady, Colin (Feb 11, 2019). "Joe Rogan Experience #1211 – Colin O'Brady." The Joe Rogan Experience (Podcast).

2   Without the sensation of a second mind or ego standing over it with a club: Watts, Alan (1957). *The Way of Zen*. New York City: Pantheon Books.

3   The Stanford Encyclopedia of Philosophy has a very thorough and insightful summary of the Zen tradition: Nagatomo, Shigenori, "Japanese Zen Buddhist Philosophy", *The Stanford Encyclopedia of Philosophy* (Spring 2020 Edition), Edward N.Zalta (ed.), forthcoming URL=<https://plato.stanford.edu/archives/spr2020/entries/japanese-zen/>.

4   Zen master Takuan Sōhō: Sōhō Takuan, & Wilson, W. S. (2012). *The unfettered mind: writings from a zen master to a master swordsman*. Boston: Shambhala.

5   Mind-wandering 47% of the time: Bradt, S. (2019, May 2). Wandering mind not a happy mind. Retrieved from https://news.harvard.edu/gazette/story/2010/11/wandering-mind-not-a-happy-mind/

6   The Last Samurai movie: The Last Samurai. Burbank, CA : Warner Home Video, 2004.

7   The Inner Game of Tennis was the first sport psychology book I read, and probably the most impactful: Gallwey, W. T. (2015). *The inner game of tennis*. London: Pan Books.

WHAT IS FLOW?

8   Maslow called flow "Peak Experiences": Maslow, A. H. (1964). *Religions, values, and peak-experiences*. Columbus: Ohio State University Press.

9   Csikszentmihalyi is widely considered as the "Godfather" of flow psychology research. Some of his works to explore:
    Csikszentmihalyi, M. (2009). *Flow: the psychology of optimal experience*. New York: Harper Row.

Csikszentmihalyi, M. (2000). *Beyond boredom and anxiety.* San Francisco: Jossey-Bass Publishers.

Csikszentmihalyi, M. (2016). *Flow and the foundations of positive psychology: the collected works of Mihaly Csikszentmihalyi.* Dordrecht: Springer.

10 **Cited in George Mumford's book:** Mumford, G. (2016). *The mindful athlete: secrets to pure performance.* Berkeley, CA: Parallax Press.

11 **Steven Kotler is a journalist and author who has greatly popularized flow science and research:**
Kotler, S. (2015). *The rise of superman: decoding the science of ultimate human performance.* London: Quercus.

Kotler, S., & Wheal, J. (2018). *Stealing fire: how Silicon Valley, the Navy SEALs, and maverick scientists are revolutionizing the way we live and work.* New York: Dey St.

His team at the Flow Research Collective are also doing amazing things. See: www.flowresearchcollective.com

12 **behind every gold medal or world championship that ever been won, there is likely a flow state behind the victory:** Quoted from Kotler, S. (2015). *The rise of superman: decoding the science of ultimate human performance.* London: Quercus.

13 **Transient Hypo-Frontality theory described in:** Dietrich, A. (2003). Functional neuroanatomy of altered states of consciousness: The transient hypofrontality hypothesis. *Consciousness and Cognition, 12*(2), 231–256.

Also see his TEDx talk: TEDX Talks (2011, November, 8). *TEDxBeirut - Arne Dietrich - Surfing the Stream of Consciousness: Tales from the Hallucination Zone [Video].* YouTube. https://www.youtube.com/watch?v=syfalikXBLA&feature=emb_title

14 **functional magnetic resonance imaging (fMRI) to examine the brains of improv jazz musicians in flow:** Johns Hopkins Medical Institutions. (2008, February 28). This Is Your Brain On Jazz: Researchers Use MRI To Study Spontaneity, Creativity. *ScienceDaily.* Retrieved February 26, 2020 from www.sciencedaily.com/releases/2008/02/080226213431.htm

15 **Dual-process theory of cognition:** Evans, J.S.B.T. (2003) In two minds: Dual-process accounts of reasoning. *Trends in Cognitive Sciences, 7*(10), 454–459

16 **Flow is System 1 doing:** Järvilehto, L. (2016). *Intuition and flow.* In L. Harmat, F. Ø. Andersen, F. Ullén, J. Wright, & G. Sadlo (Eds.), *Flow experience: Empirical research and applications* (p. 95–104). Springer International Publishing.

17 **Changes in brainwave function also occur in the brain in a state of flow:** Kotler, S. (2014, April 30). 'Flow' or Peak Performance Is Supported by Science. Retrieved from https://time.com/56809/the-science-of-peak-human-performance/

18 **flow states currently lack a systematic method of training:** Nosworthy, C. et al.

(2017). A systematic review of flow training on flow states & performance in elite athletes. Grad J of Sport, Ex & Phys Ed Res, 6, pp. 16 - 28.

19 **Flow antecedents and conditions have been extensively researched and added to, but Csikszentimihalyi's original work still holds up. The antecedents listed were taken from a summary of collective work cited in:** Csikszentmihalyi, M., Latter, P., & Duranso, C. W. (2017). *Running flow: mental immersion techniques for better running.* Champaign, IL: Human Kinetics.

    For an extensive summary of flow research see: Harmat, L., Andersen, F. Ø., Ullén, F., Wright, J., & Sadlo, G. (Eds.) (2016). Flow experience: empirical research and applications. Springer.

20 **the flow experience falls on a spectrum:** Jackson, S. A., & Csíkszentmihályi Mihály. (1999). *Flow in sports.* Champaign, IL: Human Kinetics.

21 **According to Kotler, there are 17 or more known triggers:** Kotler, S. (2015, February 27). Retrieved, from https://bigthink.com/videos/understanding-flow-triggers-with-steven-kotler

22 **Yerkes Dodson law shows a correlation between anxiety/arousal and performance. We need a certain amount of anxiety in order to drive attention which increases performance:** Yerkes, R.M, Dodson, J.D (1908). "The relation of strength of stimulus to rapidity of habit-formation." Journal of Comparative Neurology and Psychology. 18 (5): 459–482.

23 **Challenge-skill balance, clear goals, and a sense of control were found to be strong predictors:** Carlton J. Fong, Diana J. Zaleski & Jennifer Kay Leach (2015) The challenge–skill balance and antecedents of flow: A meta-analytic investigation, The Journal of Positive Psychology, 10:5, 425-446.

24 **Researchers Stefan Engeser and Falko Rheinberg found different moderators of the challenge-skill balance:** Engeser, S., & Rheinberg, F. (2008). Flow, performance and moderators of challenge-skill balance. *Motivation and Emotion, 32*(3), 158–172.

25 For a real macro-flow experience see the work of free solo climber Alex Honnold, in particular the National Geographic documentary *Free Solo* (2018).

26 **individuals that are high achievers tend to experience flow more frequently than low achievers:** Csikszentmihalyi, M. (1975). Beyond boredom and anxiety. San Francisco: Jossey-Bass

    Csikszentmihalyi, M. (1990). Flow: The psychology of optimal experience. New York: Harper & Row.

27 **studies done on chess players revealed that levels of enjoyment were the highest when playing against an opponent that was better compared to an equally ranked opponent:** Abuhamdeh, S., & Csikszentmihalyi, M. (2009). Intrinsic and extrinsic

motivational orientations in the competitive context: An examination of person-situation interactions. *Journal of Personality*, 77, 1615–1635.

28 **Achievement Goal Theory (AGT):** Duda, & Balageur, I. (2007). Coach-created motivation climate. In S. Jowett and D. Lavallee (Eds.) Social Psychology in Sport, (pp. 75-90). Champaign, Il: Human Kinetics.

29 **boost in neurochemicals like norepinephrine and dopamine:** Steven Kotler has a good overview of flow literature on the neurochemistry of flow and creativity on his website: https://www.stevenkotler.com/rabbithole/ea-ullam-copy

30 **slow is smooth, and smooth is fast:** D. Taylor, Personal communication, July 13, 2019.

31 **for the first time in my life, everything in my head finally shut up:** Adee, S. (2012, March 30). How electrical brain stimulation can change the way we think. Retrieved from https://theweek.com/articles/476866/how-electrical-brain-stimulation-change-way-think

32 **Autoletic personality:** Csikszentmihalyi, M. (1997). Finding Flow. The Psychology of engagement with everyday life. New York: Basic Books.

33 **participants sitting at home experienced twice as much anxiety, and also fewer occasions for flow:** Bassi M., Delle Fave A. (2016) Flow in the Context of Daily Experience Fluctuation. In: Harmat L., Ørsted Andersen F., Ullén F., Wright J., Sadlo G. (eds). *Flow experience: Empirical research and applications* (p.191-106). Springer International Publishing.

34 **For a comprehensive look at sport-specific flow research, see Susan Jackson and Mihaly Csikszentmihalyi's sport psychology classic, *Flow in Sports*:** Jackson, S., & Csikszentmihalyi, M. (1999). Flow in sports: The keys to optimal experiences and performances. Champaign: Human Kinetics.

35 **Flow is related to enhanced well-being and self-concept:**
Haworth, J. (1993). Skills-challenge relationships and psychological well-being in everyday life. *Society & Leisure, 16*, 115-128.
Jackson, S., Thomas, P., Marsh, H., & Smethurst, C. (2001). Relationships between fl ow, self-concept, psychological skills, and performance. Journal of Applied Sport Psychology, 13 ,129–153.

36 **studies confirm that experiencing flow is an important predictor of subjective emotional well-being and healthy aging:** Fritz, B. S., & Avsec, A. (2007). The experience of flow and subjective well-being of music students. *Psihološka Obzorja / Horizons of Psychology, 16*(2), 5–17.
Ryff, C. D., Singer, B. H., & Dienberg Love, G. (2004). Positive health: connecting well-being with biology. *Philosophical transactions of the Royal Society of London. Series*

B, Biological sciences, 359(1449), 1383–1394.

37 **concentration can facilitate the subjective experience of flow:** Mills, M., & Fullagar, C. (2008). Motivation and Flow: Toward an Understanding of the Dynamics of the Relation in Architecture Students. *The Journal of psychology: Interdisciplinary and Applied.* 142. 533-53.

38 **Self-Determination Theory:** Ryan, R. M., & Deci, E. L. (2000). Self-determination theory and the facilitation of intrinsic motivation, social development, and well-being. *American Psychologist, 55*(1), 68–78.

39 **Research has suggested that whenever an autonomy-supportive environment is nurtured, there is a greater quality of motivation:** Goudas et al., 1995 as cited in Biddle, S.J.H. & Mutrue, N. (2008). Motivation for physical activity: Introduction and overview. In S.J.H. Biddle & N. Mutrie, *Psychology of physical activity: Determinants, well-being and interventions.* London: Routledge. (pp. 39-53).

40 **People tend to prioritize enjoyment and revitalisation more than exercising for appearance and weight management:** Ingledew, D. K., Markland, D., & Medley, A. R. (1998). *Exercise motives and stages of change. Journal of Health Psychology,* 3, 477–489.

THE ROAD TO MENTAL MASTERY

41 Dr. Gervais has worked with individuals on the razor's edge of high performance and has pioneered a new wave of performance psychology. He is also the host of *Finding Mastery*, a podcast that takes a deep dive into the mechanics of pursuing mastery. I highly recommend it: https://findingmastery.net/. Be sure to check out his audiobook as well called *Compete to Create: An Approach to Living and Leading Authentically,* co-written with coach Pete Carroll.

42 **Atomic Habits:** Clear, J. (2018). *Atomic habits: an easy & proven way to build good habits & break bad ones; tiny changes, remarkable results.* New York: Avery, an imprint of Penguin Random House.

43 **10,000-hour rule:** There is still some correlation between the number of hours put in and competency, so it isn't necessarily bad advice: Gladwell, M. (2013). *Outliers: the story of success.* New York: Back Bay Books.

   Ericsson's original research: Ericsson, K. A., Krampe, R. T., & Tesch-Römer, C. (1993). The role of deliberate practice in the acquisition of expert performance. *Psychological Review, 100*(3).

44 **simplicity of expression, rather than complexity of form:** Lee, B., & Little, J. R. (2001). *Bruce Lee: artist of life.* Rutland, VT: Tuttle Publishing.

45 This concept is frequently but incorrectly attributed to Abraham Maslow. The model was first used at Gordon Training International by its employee Noel Burch in the

1970s; there it was called the "four stages for learning any new skill": Curtiss, P.R., Warren, P.W., (1973). *The dynamics of life skills coaching.* Life skills series. Prince Albert, Saskatchewan: Training Research and Development Station, Dept. of Manpower and Immigration. p. 89

46 **paralysis by analysis:** Decaro, M. S., Thomas, R. D., Albert, N. B., & Beilock, S. L. (2011). Choking under pressure: Multiple routes to skill failure. *Journal of Experimental Psychology: General, 140*(3), 390–406.

47 **researchers found that the presence of audiences impaired performance on complex tasks** (But increased performance on simpler tasks): Baron, R. S.; Moore, D. & Sanders, G. S. (1978). "Distraction as a source of drive in social facilitation research." *Journal of Personality and Social Psychology.* 36 (8): 816.

48 **Dunning-Kruger Effect:** Kruger, J., Dunning, D. (1999). Unskilled and unware of it: How difficulties in recoginzing one's own incompetence lead to inflated self-assessments. *Journal of personality and social psychology, 77*(6). 1121-1134.

49 **The Beginners Mind:** Shunryu Suzuki (2011). *Zen Mind, Beginner's Mind.* Shambhala Publications.

50 Harris, S. (2015). *Waking up: a guide to spirituality without religion.* New York: Simon & Schuster.

SELF-AWARENESS

51 **Self-actualization:** Maslow, A. H. (1943). **A theory of human motivation**. *Psychological Review, 50*(4), 370-96.

52 **High challenge =how, low challenge = why:** Höchli, B., Brügger, A., & Messner, C. (2018). How Focusing on Superordinate Goals Motivates Broad, Long-Term Goal Pursuit: A Theoretical Perspective. *Frontiers in psychology, 9*, 1879.

53 **Growth vs Fixed Mindset:** Dweck, C. S. (2008). *Mindset: the new psychology of success.* New York: Ballantine Books.

CLEAR OBJECTIVES

54 **review of the effects of goal setting on performance:** Locke, E. A., Shaw, K. N., Saari, L. M., & Latham, G. P. (1981). Goal setting and task performance: 1969–1980. *Psychological Bulletin, 90*(1), 125–152.

55 **Outcome (or ego) oriented individuals on the other hand, tend to perceive a challenge as a personal lack of ability and assess situations more unfavorably:** Tuckey, M., Brewer, N., & Williamson, P. (2002). The influence of motives and goal orientation on feedback seeking. *Journal of Occupational and Organizational Psychology, 75*(2), 195–216.

56 **100-Day Plan:** Gilson, C., Pratt, M., Roberts, K., & Weymes, E. (2000). Peak performance: Business lessons from the world's top sports organizations. London: Harper Collins Business.

57 **Performance Profiling:** Butler, R.J. & Hardy, L. (1992) The Performance Profile: Theory and Application. *The Sport Psychologist*, 6, 253-264.

58 **Though this is much debated in the scientific community, EI has shown great potential. Daniel Goleman is a pioneering researcher on the impact of EI. :** Goleman, D. (1998). *Working With Emotional Intelligence.* New York, NY. Bantum Books.

59 **EQ 360:** Weisinger, H., & Pawliw-Fry, J. P. (2015). *Performing under pressure: the science of doing your best when it matters most.* New York: Crown Business.

60 **For an overview of imagery research and use in sport, see:** Morris, T., Spittle, M., & Watt, A.P. (2005). Imagery in sport. Champaign, IL: Human Kinetics.

61 **Check out Angela Duckworth's brilliant TED talk:** Duckworth, A. (April 2013). *The power of passion and perseverance*

MINDFULNESS

62 **non-judgemental present moment awareness:** Kabat-Zinn, J. (2005). *Full catastrophe living: using the wisdom of your body and mind to face stress, pain, and illness.* New York, NY: Bantam Dell.

63 **Default Mode Network (DMN):** Garrison, K. A., Zeffiro, T. A., Scheinost, D., Constable, R. T., & Brewer, J. A. (2015). Meditation leads to reduced default mode network activity beyond an active task. *Cognitive, affective & behavioral neuroscience,* 15(3), 712–720.

64 **individuals who are put through a mindfulness-based performance enhancement program show significant increases in flow experiences:** Lutkenhouse, J., Gardner, F. L., & Morrow, C. (2007). A randomized controlled trial comparing the performance enhancement effects of Mindfulness-Acceptance-Commitment (MAC) performance enhancement and psychological skills training procedures. Manuscript in preparation.

65 **"Muddy water is best cleared by leaving it alone": *The Way of Zen:*** Watts, Alan (1957). *The Way of Zen.* New York City: Pantheon Books.

66 **meditation can possibly temper a reflexive response that is located in regions of the human nervous system:** Levenson RW, Ekman P, Ricard M. Meditation and the startle response: a case study. *Emotion.* 2012;12(3):650–658.

67 **Gamma waves:** Gilsinan, K. (2017, April 28). The Brains of the Buddhists.<https://www.the-atlantic.com/health/archive/2015/07/dalai-lama-neuroscience-compassion/397706/>

68 **four days of meditation significantly improved both creativity and cognitive flexibility:** University of North Carolina at Charlotte. (2010, April, 19). Brief meditative exercise helps cognition. *ScienceDaily.* <www.sciencedaily.com/releas­es/2010/04/100414184220.htm>.

69 **Man's Search for Meaning:** Frankl, V. E. (1984). *Man's search for meaning: An introduction to logotherapy.* New York: Simon & Schuster.

70 **Marathon monks of Mount Hiei:** Stevens, John. & Namba, Tadashi. (1989). *The marathon monks of Mount Hiei / John Stevens; photographs by Todashi Namba.* London; Sydney: Rider.

71 **Conscious breathing is my anchor:** Nhat Hanh, T. (1990). *Present Moment Wonderful Moment: Mindfulness Verses for Daily Living.* Berkeley, CA: Parallax Press.

72 **Author Robert green provides a good explanation of OODA on his blog:** Green, R. (2007, February 24). OODA and You. Retrieved from https://powerseductionandwar.com/ooda-and-you/

73 **The Guest House, from:** *Rumi: Selected Poems,* trans Coleman Barks with John Moynce, A. J. Arberry, Reynold Nicholson (Penguin Books, 2004).

74 **Zen in the Art of Archery:** Herrigel, E. (1971). *Zen in the art of archery.* New York: Vantage Books.

75 **golfers who had their brains scanned while performing a putting task...:** Crews, D. J., & Landers, D. M. (1993). Electroencephalographic measures of attentional patterns prior to the golf putt. *Medicine & Science in Sports & Exercise, 25*(1), 116–126.

76 **The elephant and the rider:** Haidt, J. (2006). The happiness hypothesis: Finding modern truth in ancient wisdom. New York: Basic Books.

GROUP FLOW

77 **Social flow is more enjoyable:** Walker, Charles. (2010). Experiencing Flow: Is Doing it Together Better Than Doing it Alone? The Journal of Positive Psychology. 5. 3-11.

78 **Collective effervescence:** Carls, P. (n.d.). Émile Durkheim, Internet Encyclopedia of Philosophy. Retrieved from https://www.iep.utm.edu/durkheim/

79 **The ballet of surgery:** In Csikszentmihalyi, M. (2009). Flow: the psychology of optimal experience. New York: Harper Row. p. 65.

80 **people who participated in group flow were the highest performers:** Cross, R., & Parker, A. (2004). Charged up: Creating energy in organizations. Journal of Organizational Excellence, 3-14.

81 **Keith Sawyer studied under Csikszentmihalyi and build upon his original work. Check out his book for a great breakdown of group flow conditions:** Sawyer, K. (2007). Group genius: The creative power of collaboration. Basic Books.

82 **Psychological Safety:** Delizonna, L. (n.d). High-Performing Teams Need Psychological Safety. Here's How to Create It. Harvard Business Review.

83 **Agreement leads to cohesion:** Hackman, J.R., Wageman, R., Ruddy, T.M., Ray, C.R., Cooper, C.D., & Locke, E.A. (2000). Team effectiveness in theory and practice. In *Industrial and Organizational Psychology: Theory and Practise*, ed. Cooper C, Locke, E.A, Oxford, UK: Blackwell publishers.

84 **Group cohesion:** Carron, Albert & Colman, Michelle & Wheeler, Jennifer & Stevens, Diane. (2002). Cohesion and performance in sport: A meta-analysis. Journal of Sport & Exercise Psychology. 24. 168-188.

85 **Cohesion-performance relationship:** Mullen, B., & Copper, C. (1994). The relation between group cohesiveness and performance: An integration. *Psychological Bulletin,* 115(2), 210–227.

86 **Group Environment Questionnaire (GEQ):** Carron, A. V., Widmeyer, W. N., & Brawley, L. R. (1985). The development of an instrument to assess cohesion in sport teams: The Group Environment Questionnaire. Journal of Sport Psychology, 7, 244-266.

87 **Flow Short Scale (FSS):** Rheinberg, F., Vollmeyer, R., & Engeser, S. (2003). Die Erfassung des Flow-Erlebens [The assessment of flow experience]. In J. Stiensmeier-Pelster & F. Rheinberg (Eds.), Diagnostik von Selbstkonzept, Lernmotivation und Selbstregulation [Diagnosis of motivation and self-concept], 261–279: Gottingen: Hogrefe.

88 During my studies I had an opportunity to explore this relationship as it relates to flow: The paper is not peer-reviewed, so take it with a grain of salt: Komar, M.T (2016). *Measuring Flow in Team Environments: The Role of Group Cohesion and Leadership* Style on the Susceptibility of the Flow State. (Master's thesis). Lund University, Lund, Sweden.

89 **teams that have higher interdependent tasks have been shown to experience group flow more frequently:** Charles J. Walker (2010). Experiencing flow: Is doing it together better than doing it alone? The Journal of Positive Psychology, 5:1, 3-11. Steiner, I. D. (1972). *Group process and productivity.* New York: Academic Press.

90 **Challenge-Support matrix for training mental fortitude:** David Fletcher & Mustafa Sarkar (2016) Mental fortitude training: An evidence-based approach to developing psychological resilience for sustained success, Journal of Sport Psychology in Action, 7:3, 135-157.

THE BURNOUT GENERATION

91 **Altered states economy:** Kotler, S., & Wheal, J. (2017). *Stealing fire: how Silicon Valley, the Navy SEALS, and maverick scientists are revolutionizing the way we live and work.*

First edition. New York, NY: Dey St., an imprint of William Morrow.

92 **Dark side of flow:** Hogarth, Brent (2018). Shining Light on the Dark Side of Flow: Is Mindfulness in High-Flow-State Athletes Predictive of Improved Emotion-Regulation and Self-Control? PhD Dissertation.

93 **For a look at the relationship between neurochemicals such as norepinephrine and flow, see Herbert Benson's work out of Harvard:** Benson, H. (2003). *The Breakout Principle How to Activate the Natural Trigger That Maximizes Creativity, Athletic Performance, Productivity and Personal Well-being.* Scribner.

    Steven Kotler and the Flow Genome Project expand on Herbert Benson's work. See: Big Think. (2015, October, 15). *Hack Your Flow: Understanding Flow Cycles, with Steven Kotler. [Video].* https://www.youtube.com/watch?v=JWy_cBcawKQ

94 **Overspecialization leads to higher rates of injuries.** For more on this and other sport myths debunked, check out David Epstein's book: Epstein, D. J. (2013). *The sports gene: what makes the perfect athlete.* London: Yellow Jersey Press.

    Also see: "Can you guess the one thing that most elite athletes have in common?" https://activeforlife.com/what-elite-athletes-have-in-common/,

    "The downside of year-round hockey: Ottawa Senators strength coach warns of declining athleticism among youth" https://nationalpost.com/sports/hockey/nhl/the-downside-of-year-round-hockey-ottawa-senators-strength-coach-warns-of-declining-athleticism-among-youth,

    "The Late-Bloomer Advantage in Sports" https://www.huffpost.com/entry/the-latebloomer-advantage_b_9823272

95 O'Sullivan, J. (2017, November 15). Can you guess the one thing that most elite athletes have in common? [Blog Post]. Retrieved from https://activeforlife.com/what-elite-athletes-have-in-common/

96 **Greater adherence to exercise programs for example, was found with instructors who fostered an autonomy-supportive environment:** Biddle, S.J.H., Hagger, M.s., Chatzisarantis, N.L.D., & Lippke, S. (2007). Theoretical frameworks in exercise psychology. In G. Tenenbaum & R. Eklund (Eds.), Handbook for sport psychology (3rd ed., pp. 5370559). Hoboken, NJ: Wiley.

PROTECT YOUR ATTENTION

97 **a wealth of information creates a poverty of attention:** Simon, H. A. (1971) "Designing Organizations for an Information-Rich World" in: Martin Greenberger, Computers, *Communication, and the Public Interest, Baltimore.* MD: The Johns Hopkins Press. pp. 40–41.

98 **studies show that sharing your exercise with others on social media can improve**

motivation to exercise: Divine, A., Watson, P.M., Baker, S., Hall, C.R. (2019). Facebook, relatedness and exercise motivation in University students: A mixed methods investigation. Computer in Human Behavior, Volume 91. pp. 138-150.

99 **Sharing your intentions with other people can reduce likelihood of goal achieve-ment:** Gollwitzer, P. M., Sheeran, P., Michalski, V., & Seifert, A. E. (2009). When Intentions Go Public: Does Social Reality Widen the Intention-Behavior Gap? *Psychological Science, 20*(5), 612–618.

LIVE SLOW, FIND FLOW

100 **Self-actualization vs self-image actualization:** Lee, B., & Little, J. R. (1999). *Bruce Lee: Artist of life*. Boston: Tuttle Pub.

101 Smith, M. M., Sherry, S. B., Vidovic, V., Saklofske, D. H., Stoeber, J., & Benoit, A. (2019). Perfectionism and the Five-Factor Model of Personality: A Meta-Analytic Review. *Personality and Social Psychology Review, 23*(4), 367–390.

Sherry, S. & Smith, M. (2019, February 5). Young people drowning in a rising tide of perfectionism. Retrieved from http://theconversation.com/young-people-drowning-in-a-rising-tide-of-perfectionism-110343

About the Author

Marek Komar, MMSc., MSc. is a Mental Performance Consultant and long-time athlete on the journey of mental mastery. He is the founder of Flow Performance, a performance psychology consultancy with the mission of increasing the amount of time people spend in flow by empowering individuals and teams with the necessary mental skills to perform at their best.

Marek seeks to understand one fundamental question: What is holding you back from performing at your best? From his own experiences as a high-level athlete he understood that for him, it was his mental game. He has coached athletes and teams on how to get out of their own way and reach their optimal performance. Marek has worked with various individuals, teams, and organizations (including, but not limited to sport) helping to enhance mental performance and group dynamics. Notable clients include University athletes and teams, Team Canada athletes, CFL champions, Olympic hopefuls, as well as Special Olympics athletes and coaches.

When he is not annoying his clients with "Yoda" quotes, he enjoys staying competitive and healthy playing soccer and trail running. He holds a Kinesiology degree specializing in Sports Performance from the University of Alberta, a Master of Medical Science specializing in Sport Psychology from Lund University (Sweden), as well as a Master of Sport Science in Diagnostics and Intervention from Leipzig University (Germany). Marek is also a professional member of the Canadian Sport Psychology Association (CSPA). He resides in Edmonton, Alberta, Canada.

www.ingramcontent.com/pod-product-compliance
Lightning Source LLC
Chambersburg PA
CBHW020252030426
42336CB00010B/734